*Praise for*

# The Magnificent World of Spirits

"Years ago, my philosophy professor at the Berkeley campus of the University of California sometimes asked his students that if there existed a life after death, why hadn't anyone ever returned to tell about it. Not too many years later the Gallop polling service announced that according to a recent survey as many as six million Americans claimed to have had near-death experiences in which they had died, gone to a spirit world, then returned to their earthly bodies and tell about it. I'm sure that number is much higher today.

"Since death lurks on the horizon for all of us, if not sooner, then later, shouldn't we be more than a little curious about what will happen when that light in our minds and hearts finally goes out? The content from millions of near-death experiences presents a more than compelling argument that life is not snuffed out at death, but continues in a world of spirits.

"Jesus said in His father's house there are many mansions. The spirit world is a land of education and music, a vast and wonderful place with beautiful towns and cities, clean rivers, green forests and vast mountains with animals of every kind living in lush and beautiful gardens. There are radiant palaces and large assembly halls, with education programs for people at all levels of progression. Many of the communities will be found in a place called paradise, while others are confined to a spirit prison area where Earth's trouble makers struggle with the more basic lessons that must be learned to get along in this world and the next.

"Deceased family members from countless generations get to know each other as they organize into family organizations. Some of us will be allowed to return to earth life, as guardian angels, to assist our friends and loved ones. I sure hope I get to do some of that.

"Others will teach how the mission of Jesus Christ binds us all together into one huge eternal family, how we are progressing toward a glorious resurrection with perfect bodies, and how we are are preparing to function in a universe containing worlds without number. We will remember the premortal existence where all of us lived before coming to earth.

"In her new book, *The Magnificent World of Spirits*, Marlene Bateman Sullivan describes in detail the world we will all enter after death; what we will see, whom we will be with, and what we will likely be doing. Her information comes from hundreds of near death accounts, the scriptures, and the words of prophets and sages; a culmination of years of research.

"I suppose Marlene could have titled this work *The Door of Death*, a handbook for those who wish to be better prepared, less taken by surprise, and less overwhelmed during those hours and days following the moment of death. None of us know exactly when death will be at the door. Why not prepare now? Read Marlene's book."

—Lee Nelson, author of *Visions from Beyond the Veil* and many other titles

# the Magnificent WORLD of Spirits

# the
# Magnificent
# WORLD
# of Spirits

### EYEWITNESS
### ACCOUNTS
### *of where we go*
### WHEN
### WE DIE

## MARLENE BATEMAN
# SULLIVAN

CFI
An Imprint of Cedar Fort, Inc.
Springville, Utah

ISBN 13: 978-1-4621-1778-9

Published by CFI, an imprint of Cedar Fort, Inc.
2373 W. 700 S., Springville, UT 84663
Distributed by Cedar Fort, Inc., www.cedarfort.com

Library of Congress Cataloging-in-Publication Data

Sullivan, Marlene Bateman, author.
The magnificent world of spirits / Marlene Bateman Sullivan.
    pages cm
Includes bibliographical references.
ISBN 978-1-4621-1778-9 (perfect bound : alk. paper)
1. Future life--Church of Jesus Christ of Latter-day Saints. 2. Future life--Mormon
Church. 3. Death--Religious aspects--Church of Jesus Christ of Latter-day Saints.
4. Death--Religious aspects--Mormon Church. 5. Near-death experiences--Religious
aspects--Church of Jesus Christ of Latter-day Saints. 6. Near-death experiences--Reli-
gious aspects--Mormon Church. 7. Church of Jesus Christ of Latter-day Saints--Doc-
trines. 8. Mormon Church--Doctrines. I. Title.

BX8643.F87S854 2015
236'.2--dc23

2015032941

Cover design by Shawnda T. Craig
Cover design © 2016 Cedar Fort, Inc.
Typeset by Jessica B. Ellingson

Printed in the United States of America

10  9  8  7  6  5  4  3  2  1

Printed on acid-free paper

To dear Ali

# Contents

# Foreword

## Knowledge Is to Be Poured Down from Heaven

Hindsight is a wonderful thing—a truly great blessing! Looking back from a 2016 perspective, it becomes obvious that God has poured out a great blessing on all this earth's inhabitants. He has changed millions of minds and hearts and has opened up a vast new area of understanding and knowledge worldwide.

For many centuries, the thought that a mortal could communicate with those who are "dead" was a major religious and social taboo. Many centuries ago, the Inquisition dealt relentlessly with those who claimed to have received spirit-world communications. Centuries later, people were burned as witches for asserting that they had received otherworld visitations. Even in the "more enlightened" twentieth century, many of those who shared such experiences were regarded as liars, deceived, odd, strange, or peculiar and often were told by religious leaders or family members not to share such things with others. Many who had received beyond-the-veil communications recorded the experiences in their personal journals but didn't speak of them, even to most of their family members.

During the past six or seven decades, those social mores have undergone a major worldwide shift. That change apparently is one of the significant changes the Lord has brought about as one of the many changes occurring in this dispensation of the "restitution of all things."

It is obvious that He has opened the doorways of "accessibility" and "respectability" for many thousands who have experienced beyond-the-veil communications. No longer is it regarded as improper for recipients of those beyond-the-veil experiences or communications to share those remarkable experiences with others. The time has come when it is appropriate, and commonplace, for such experiences to be shared with others and even published and widely disseminated. Knowledge of what awaits those who leave this mortal existence and enter the spirit world is increasingly available worldwide.

## Books on Spirit World Experiences Enabled a Worldwide Change of Social Mores

How did this come to pass? It's interesting to examine the publication dates of books that contributed to the dissemination of these life-after-death experiences. Hindsight now shows that *Life Everlasting*, a book written primarily for Latter-day Saint readers, was an early catalyst in the process. It quickly reached bestseller status and sold over 100,000 copies in the first two years—before the other books listed below began to come into print. That, apparently, was one of the reasons Latter-day Saints were so accepting of the many books on the subject that followed—their minds had been opened and prepared.

After *Life Everlasting* was published in 1967, it was soon followed by other significant books on the subject. In 1969, Dr. Elizabeth Kübler-Ross published *On Death and Dying*, the first of several volumes she wrote relating to the death experience. In 1975, Dr. Raymond A. Moody Jr. released *Life After Life,* which caught the attention of the nation, became a national bestseller, made the subject even more popular, and opened the way for numerous other studies. In 1978, George W. Ritchie published an account of his near-death experience, *Return From Tomorrow*, which was widely read in this era.

Numerous other books on the subject began flowing to both national and international audiences: 1979, *Beyond Death's Door* by Maurice Rawlings; 1980, *Life at Death* by Kenneth Ring; 1982, *Adventures in Immortality* by George Gallup Jr.; 1982, *A Collection of Near-Death Research Readings* by Craig R. Lundahl; 1982, *Recollections of Death* by Michael B. Sabom; 1984, *Heading Toward Omega* by Kenneth Ring; 1984, *On the Other Side of Life* by Evelyn Elsaesser Valarino; 1987, *The After Death Experience* by Ian Wilson; 1987, *Otherworld Journeys* by Carol Zaleski; 1988, *Coming Back to Life* by P. M. H. Atwater; 1990, *Closer to the Light* by Melvin Morse; 1990, *Heaven and Hell* by Emanuel Swedenborg; 1991, *My Life After Dying* by George G. Ritchie; 1992, *Transformed by the Light* by Melvin Morse; and hundreds more to many audiences and in many languages by authors throughout the world.

## LDS Authors Wrote about After-Life Experiences

LDS authors eventually jumped onto the publishing bandwagon with collections of life-after-death and other spirit-world experiences. Notable among these books were 1988, *Beyond the Veil Vol. 1* by Lee Nelson; 1992, *Glimpses of Eternity* by Arvin S. Gibson; 1993, *Beyond Death's Door* by Brent L. and Wendy C. Top; 1994, *Coming from the Light* by Sarah Hinze; 1997, *I Saw Heaven!* by Lawrence E. Tooley; 1997, *The Eternal Journey* by Craig R. Lundwall and Harold A. Widdison; 1998, *The L.D.S. Gospel of Light* by B. Grant Bishop; and 2004, *Trailing Clouds of Glory* by Harold A. Widdison. Several of these LDS authors, like the other authors listed above and other LDS authors, published other books on the same subjects.

A significant result of these widely disseminated works is that people, worldwide, became aware that millions have had life-after-death and spirit-world experiences. No longer was it "strange" to have a near-death experience, and no longer did it feel necessary to keep such experiences secret for fear of being branded odd, a sensationalist, a liar, or a dreamer who couldn't distinguish fantasy from reality.

Now, fewer near-death accounts are circulated anonymously. Evidence is easier to gather. More patterns are evident. The commonality of near-death experiences between people of all nations, races, and religions removed their experiences from the realm of "secret" to the realm of knowledge, which is available to all and which is a legitimate field for personal, clinical, and scholarly study and research.

## Why Is This Great Change So Significant?

The prophet Nephi, back about 600 BC, observed that "the Lord knoweth all things from the beginning; wherefore, *he prepareth a way to accomplish all his works among the children of men*; for behold, he hath all power unto the fulfilling of all his words" (1 Nephi 9:6; emphasis added). Concurrent with this great knowledge expansion about spirit-world activities is the phenomenal expansion of genealogical work and temple work for the dead. Great technological advances have simplified the work of gathering historical data. Numerous indexes have been found and digitized so they are computer-accessible. Without a doubt, the many near-death and life-after-death experiences being made known have served to stimulate interest in preparing family records for temple covenants and ordinances to be performed for deceased relatives.

I can't speak for other authors of books on the subject, but I can tell you of my experience as the author of *Life Everlasting*. It became apparent to me, as time went by after it was published and began being widely read, that *Life Everlasting* was known by those who now reside beyond the veil. In more than a dozen instances, over the years, I have been told by individual recipients or their close family members of communications they have received beyond the veil, counseling them to obtain and read the book. On several particular occasions, they were even instructed to read a specific account, on a particular page, because it held an answer for a question or need the person was trying to resolve.

Doctrine and Covenants 121:26–33 speaks of "knowledge . . . to be revealed in the last times, . . . a time to come in the which nothing shall be withheld," a time to come when nothing shall "hinder the Almighty from pouring down knowledge from heaven."

## The Writings of Marlene Bateman Sullivan

After the turn of the century, various scholars began to focus on particular segments of knowledge concerning spirit-world scenarios, events, and practices.

And that is where the writings of Marlene Bateman Sullivan enter the picture. She is a talented, careful, scholarly, energetic author. Her writings are interesting to read, easy to follow, and full of interesting and valuable information. Besides the books I'll mention below, she has written several books chronicling experiences of various LDS heroes and heroines—books that make for interesting and testimony-building reading.

As president and senior editor of Horizon Publishers & Distributors, Inc., it was my privilege to edit and publish her first two books written for an LDS audience. They are, in 2001, *And There Were Angels Among Them: Spiritual Visitations in Early Church History*; and, in 2002, *Visits from Beyond the Veil: True Stories of Angelic Visitations*. Both are good books!

Our personal mission and other obligations caused us to merge Horizon Publishers with Cedar Fort, Inc., in 2004, so CFI has continued as the publisher for her later works. The first of her books they published continued with the angels theme: 2006, *By the Ministering of Angels*.

Her interests then expanded to cover the broader field of near-death experiences. In 2013, her book *Gaze Into Heaven: Near-Death Experiences in Early Church History* was published.

Now, in 2016, her next book on the subject is ready for publication: *The Magnificent World of Spirits: Eyewitness Accounts of Where We Go When We Die.* I count it a privilege to be asked to write this brief foreword for the book.

For your information, I've read all five of the manuscripts for these books. She's furnished you readers with loads of valuable information. You'll learn from her writings, just as I have learned from them too.

It has been a distinct pleasure to be invited to write this brief introduction in her honor.

Duane S. Crowther

*Chapter One*

# There Is No Death

AT NO TIME in life do we come so close to the infinite as at birth and at death. With birth, we enter mortality, and with death, we leave it. However, since none of us has died, the transition to the next life remains an unfamiliar and unknown experience. Exactly what happens when we die? We know our spirits will live on and go to the spirit world, but what is it like there? How will our spirit bodies be different than our physical bodies? What do people do in the spirit world? Will we be reunited with our departed loved ones? The answers to these and other questions are best answered by those who have actually visited the spirit world, and their stories are found in this book.

To the world, dying is a mystery, but because of the restored gospel, we know that after our physical bodies are laid to rest in the earth, we will return to our Father's presence. Job asked, "If a man die, shall he live again?" (Job 14:14). Jesus Christ answered, "Because I live, ye shall live also" (John 14:19). When the Savior came to earth, died, and rose again, He opened the doors of salvation to all mankind, breaking the bands of death so that we might live.

Through revelation given to modern and ancient prophets, God has told us what will happen to our spirits when we die. One of the most comforting assurances comes from Alma, who stated, "The spirits of all men, as soon as they are departed from this mortal body, yea, the spirits of all men, whether they be good or evil, are taken home to that God who gave them life" (Alma 40:11).

Death is merely a doorway that leads into the next life—a necessary step in our eternal progression. Instead of being the end, death is merely a temporary separation of our spirit and our physical body and is actually a beginning—another step forward in Heavenly Father's plan for us. At some future point when we are resurrected, our spirit and body will be reunited—never to be separated again.

Reading the experiences of people who have seen into the spirit world allows us to benefit from their knowledge and insights, which can help us make more productive use of our time on earth. These experiences teach us that our moments on earth are just that—moments—and that eternity stretches before us. The best thing we can do while here is direct our time and energy toward what really matters—our life *after* mortality.

These accounts are presented as they were written and many contain mistakes in spelling, capitalization, punctuation, and grammar. I did not "modernize" these errors because I wanted to present the material in its original form and in the writer's own words—without imposing any interpretation on their personal and sacred experiences.

Many of these experiences contain similar elements. If you would like to study specific themes, see the appendix at the back of the book, which lists each element and which experiences mention that particular element.

## Death—The Beginning of Eternal Life

Church doctrine teaches us that death is not the end and that life continues on beyond the grave. President Spencer W. Kimball said, "To the unbeliever it [death] is the end of all, associations terminated, relationships ended, memories soon to fade into nothingness. But to those who have knowledge and faith in the promise of the gospel of Jesus Christ, death's meaning is . . . a change of condition into a wider serener sphere of action; it means the beginning of eternal life."[1]

People are often afraid of death, but this usually arises from a fear of the unknown. The experiences in *The Magnificent World of Spirits* can quell that fear because it allows us to see vicariously into the spirit world—a place we will all go. These stories are valuable because they enlarge our knowledge of God and His plan for us. Learning about what lies ahead will give us a better understanding of our life on earth and how we can use the time we have to prepare for the next life.

Mortality is only an embryo state, a preparation for the eternities, and death is a necessary transition to our future state. Death is actually a deliverance, not a demise, and can be thought of as the gateway to immortality. The scriptures assure us that our spirits will live on. "Then shall the dust return to the earth as it was: and the spirit shall return unto God who gave it" (Ecclesiastes 12:7).

The English poet Samuel T. Coleridge said, "Death but supplies the oil for the inextinguishable lamp of life."[2] It is the will of God that our mortal bodies are laid in the grave when it is time for the soul to enter into the next step of our existence.

Death is simply another phase of our existence—we can think of it as stepping through an open door into another room. Knowing that death is not the end and that it plays an important part in our eternal existence will help us put this event into a proper perspective.

Brigham Young said, "We shall turn round and look upon it [death] and think, when we have crossed it, why this is the greatest advantage of my whole existence, for I have passed from a state of sorrow, grief, mourning, woe, misery, pain, anguish and disappointment into a state of existence where I can enjoy life to the fullest extent as far as that can be done without a body."[3]

## Faint Remembrances of Our Premortal Life

Before mortality, we lived with God, and when we came to earth, we not only left our home but also forgot all about it. At birth, a veil was drawn over our minds, but despite that shield, an inner flame continues to burn within our souls. This flame affirms many truths and helps us realize that our spirits are eternal, that this earth is not our natural home, that God is our Father, and that He loves us with a perfect love.

At times during mortality, we may have vague, half-defined recollections of living in our premortal existence. For many, singing the hymn "O My Father" causes a luminous nostalgia to course though our veins as our past is brought to the forefront. Other times, we may feel unexplainable sensations that let us know we are experiencing something we have felt before. There might be unaccountable reverberations in our emotions when we hear a phrase, listen to a speaker, read a particular scripture, or hear a certain hymn. These feelings testify to our premortal existence and to the holy and divine nature of our beings.

Likewise, reading the experiences in this book may trigger an echo in your soul, causing you to experience a faint, haunting recollection of what your life used to be. Besides providing us with a remembrance of the past, these stories can give us glimpses into a reality that lies ahead of us. They can comfort our souls with the knowledge that in the next life we will live in a sphere governed by love and light, a place of great beauty and everlasting peace, because it is a place where God dwells. The experiences contained in these pages bear witness that the spirit world is a place where we once lived and where we can live again if we choose to follow our Savior, Jesus Christ.

## Where Is the Spirit World?

The spirit world is closer than we think. Brigham Young once asked, "Where is the spirit world?" He then answered his own question, saying, "It is right here. . . . Do they [our spirits] go beyond the boundaries of this organized earth? No, they do not. They are brought forth upon this earth, for the express purpose of inhabiting it to all eternity. Where else are you going? No where else, only as you may be permitted. . . . If the Lord would permit it, and it was His will that it should be done, you could see the spirits that have departed from this world, as plainly as you now see bodies with your natural eyes."[4]

The Prophet Joseph Smith also testified that the spirit world is close. When speaking of departed loved ones, Joseph said, "They are not far from us."[5]

Even though the spirit world is nearby, we as mortals cannot see that sphere because the veil over our eyes renders it invisible. To discern people or objects in the spirit world, a person must be quickened, the veil must be withdrawn, and the organs of sight and hearing must be transformed.

Speaking of the spirit world, Parley P. Pratt said, "As to its location, it is here on the very planet where we were born; or, in other words, the earth and other planets of a like sphere, have their inward or spiritual spheres, as well as their outward, or temporal. The one is peopled by temporal tabernacles, and the other by spirits. A veil is drawn between the one sphere and the other, whereby all the objects in the spiritual sphere are rendered invisible to those in the temporal."[6]

## Personal Revelation

Although we cannot see the spirit world in its totality while on earth, Heavenly Father will help guide us through our lives and inspire us through personal revelation. God communicates with His children in a number of ways. Heartfelt prayer leads to personal revelation, which is facilitated through the gift of the Holy Ghost. God can also reveal His will to us in the form of dreams or visions. Apostle James E. Talmage said, "Visions and dreams have constituted a means of communication between God and men in every dispensation of the priesthood."[7]

President Harold B. Lee said, "Now there's one more way by which revelations may come, and that is by dreams. . . . I fear that in this age of sophistication there are those of us who are prone to rule out all dreams as of no purpose, and of no moment. And yet all through the scriptures there were recorded incidents where the Lord, by dreams, has directed His people."[8]

In the Old Testament, an angel told Jacob in a dream that he should return to Canaan (Genesis 31:11–13). Gideon became a hero when, after interpreting an old man's dream, he delivered Israel from the Midianites (Judges 7:13–25). When Solomon prayed for an understanding heart so he could judge the people, the Lord appeared in a dream and granted his request (1 Kings 3:5–12). Most of the book of Ezekiel is spent describing the countless visions and revelations he received from God.

In the New Testament, an angel appeared to Joseph in a dream, telling him that Mary had conceived through the power of the Holy Ghost (Matthew 1:20). After the Wise Men visited the baby Jesus, they were warned by God in a dream not to return to Herod but to use a different route when traveling back to their own country (Matthew 2:12).

Lehi had one of the most significant dreams in the Book of Mormon about the tree of life, which gives us a greater understanding of the plan of salvation (1 Nephi 8:2–38).

Apostle George F. Richards (father of the beloved Apostle LeGrand Richards) was President of the Council of the Twelve when he stated, "I believe in dreams, brethren . . . The Lord has given me dreams which to me are just as real and as much from God as was the dream of King Nebuchadnezzar, which was the means of saving a nation from starvation, or the dream of Lehi who through a dream led his colony out of the old country across the mighty deep to this promised land, or any other dreams that we might read in the scriptures." Elder Richards further declared, "The Lord has revealed to men by dreams something more than I ever understood or felt before. It is not out of place for us to have important dreams."[9]

## This Life Is a Time to Prepare

The experiences in this book teach us that now is the time to get ready for the next life. When we were fetuses developing inside our mothers' womb, our organs slowly developed to prepare us to live in mortality. Then at birth we began developing our spiritual capacities, which will prepare us to live in the world to come. Our earthly lives will provide us with a necessary and useful foundation, and in the next life, we will continue to learn and progress.

By learning the lessons these experiences impart, we can focus on what truly matters and cultivate proper priorities that will lead us back into God's presence, where we can bask in His perfect love forever. If we are wise, we will use this earthly life to prepare for the next, because where we will be in the hereafter depends on what we do now. "Treasure these things up in your hearts, and let the solemnities of eternity rest upon your minds" (D&C 43:34). By treasuring up these experiences and using them to benefit ourselves, we will be better prepared to live, die, and move on to our next estate.

Knowing what comes after this life can help us resist Satan and make it easier to bear our present-day trials and tribulations. As Amulek counseled, "Be watchful unto prayer continually, that ye may not be led away by the temptations of the devil. . . . I would exhort you to have patience, and that ye bear with all manner of afflictions; . . . but that ye have patience, and bear with those afflictions, with a firm hope that ye shall one day rest from all your afflictions" (Alma 34:39–41).

Those who visited the spirit world saw glories revealed and blessings poured out upon the righteous. The things they witnessed sank into their minds, giving them a desire to prepare for their future. Likewise, these experiences can expand our understanding of what lies ahead and can influence us to use our time wisely and make good choices that will benefit us in the next life. We can gain many blessings if we allow these stories to influence us to show more love, be more kind, be less judgmental, overcome our faults, gain knowledge, and spend more time serving others. These are the qualities that will follow us into the next life.

Reading the accounts of those who have been in the spirit world gives us valuable knowledge that can enrich our lives and bring us joy, peace, and comfort by helping us comprehend more fully the bigger picture of our eternal existence. The gospel of Jesus Christ teaches us about living and helps prepare us for the next life by helping us master and improve ourselves. In the end, the only thing that counts in the next life is how well we followed Jesus Christ in this one. We would do well to use the time allotted us to discover our purpose in life and focus our attention on the things that matter most.

## A Subject We Ought to Study More Than Any Other

The Doctrine and Covenants counsels us to learn about all things. We are told to study "things both in heaven and in the earth, and under the earth; things which have been, things which are, things which must shortly come to pass" (D&C 88:79).

The Prophet Joseph Smith urged the Saints to study about the next life in order to learn more about the purpose of their existence. He said, "All men know that they must die. And it is important that we should understand the reasons and causes of our exposure to the vicissitudes of life and of death, and the designs and purposes of God in our coming into the world, our sufferings here, and our departure hence. What is the object of our coming into existence, then dying and falling away, to be here no more? It is but reasonable to suppose that God would reveal something in reference to the matter, and it is a subject we ought to study more than any other. We ought to study it day and night, for the world is ignorant in reference to their true condition and relation. If we have any claim on our Heavenly Father for anything, it is for knowledge on this important subject. . . . Could you gaze into heaven five minutes, you would know more than you would by reading all that ever was written on the subject."[10]

It is only right to want to understand more about all phases of our existence, including our life prior to mortality and what awaits us after mortality. As we study and learn, we will come to understand that life in the spirit world is simply be an extension of our mortal lives. Such knowledge can comfort us in times of sorrow, teach us the true nature of our existence, and help us better comprehend God's purposes.

Studying about the hereafter means more than just reading— it means taking the time and effort to search, ponder, and learn. If we want to spend the rest of our eternal lives in a place of glory, we need to use this life to prepare for it by working to better ourselves and by learning all we can.

Although members of The Church of Jesus Christ of Latter-day Saints are already familiar with the concepts and doctrine contained in the plan of salvation, reading the experiences in *The Magnificent World of Spirits* will enhance our understanding of this plan. Studying these experiences can be enlightening and give us a better understanding not only about this life but about the life to come. There is a wealth of information contained in these personal glimpses into the spirit world, which can help us gain crucial insights about our life in mortality and allow us to redirect our energy to what really matters—the eternity that lies before us.

"Ye worlds of light and life, beyond our sphere;
Mysterious country! let your light appear.
Ye angels, lift the veil, the truth unfold,
And give our Seers a glimpse of that bright world;
Tell where ye live, and what is your employ,
Your present blessing, and your future joy."[11]

# Notes

1.  Edward Kimball, (compiled and edited), *The Teachings of Spencer W. Kimball* (Salt Lake City: Bookcraft, 1982), 39.

2.  Samuel Taylor Coleridge, *The Table Talk and Omniana of Samuel Taylor Coleridge*, ed. T. Ashe (London: George Bell and Sons, 1884), 410.

3.  Brigham Young, *Journal of Discourses* vol. 17 (London: Latter-day Saints' Book Depot, 1875), 142.

4.  Brigham Young, *Journal of Discourses,* vol. 3 (London: Latter-day Saints' Book Depot, 1856), 369.

5.  Joseph Smith, *History of the Church, Period 1*, vol. 6, (Salt Lake City: The Church of Jesus Christ of Latter-day Saints, 1843), 52.

6.  Parley P. Pratt, *Key to the Science of Theology*, 5th ed, (Salt Lake City: Deseret Book, 1891), 132–3.

7.  James E. Talmage, *A Study of the Articles of Faith*, (Salt Lake City: Church of Jesus Christ of Latter-day Saints, 1924), 226.

8.  *Teachings of Presidents of the Church: Harold B. Lee.* (Salt Lake City: The Church of Jesus Christ of Latter-day Saints, 2000), 51.

9.  George F. Richards, as quoted by Spencer W. Kimball in Conference Report, April 1974, 173.

10. Joseph Smith, *History of the Church, Period I,* vol. 6, (Salt Lake City: The Church of Jesus Christ of Latter-day Saints, 9 October, 1843), 50.

11. Parley P. Pratt, *Key to the Science of Theology,* 5th ed. (Salt Lake City: Deseret Book, 1891), 131.

*Chapter Two*

# Leaving Mortality

*J*OSEPH F. SMITH said, "Man is a dual being, composed of the spirit which gives life, force, intelligence and capacity to man, and the body which is the tenement of the spirit."[1] Death occurs when the physical body, weakened by disease or age or injured by sudden trauma, is no longer able to sustain the spirit, which then leaves. The spirit then moves to the spirit world to dwell until the resurrection, when it will be reunited with the physical body.

Brigham Young said, "Our bodies are composed of visible, tangible matter. . . . What is commonly called death does not destroy the body, it only causes a separation of spirit and body, but the principle of life, inherent in the native elements, of which the body is composed, still continues."[2]

## The Spirit Views Its Physical Body

Typically, the first thing that occurs at death is the spirit rising out of the physical body. In most cases, the person will look at their physical body before departing. In near-death experiences, it's a frequent occurrence for people to gaze down and see their body before proceeding to the spirit world.³ Newly departed spirits don't exhibit any sadness or fear at seeing their body, indicating they intuitively understand that the mortal body is only a shell.

## Ruby Lee Vaughn

When Ruby Lee Vaughn visited the spirit world, she paused briefly to look back at her physical body. Ruby tells about her experience as follows.

"An experience which I hold very sacred happened to me at my home, 127 Vidas Avenue in Salt Lake City on August 5th, 1928. When I returned home after working at a root beer stand at 12:15, the words of the song, 'Have I Done Any Good in the World Today?' ran through my mind and I strongly felt the spirit of the Lord with me as I knelt to pray. Never have I felt so humble and close to my Heavenly Father! I really prayed with all my heart and soul.

"I no sooner rose and got settled in bed than I heard a voice call 'Ruby.' I thought it must have been my sister Elma, so I went to her room and asked if she had called me. She told me she hadn't so I woke my sister Katherine and she too said she had not called me. Feeling somewhat frightened, I went back to bed. No sooner was I settled down than I heard my name called again. I was puzzled and troubled, because I knew that the voice had come from somewhere in the house, so I got up enough courage to wake my parents and ask them; mother had been working hard and was very tired, but they both said no. When my brother also said 'No.' to me, I was concerned, but went to bed, knowing that I had heard my name called twice.

"As soon as I was once more settled in bed, I again heard a voice call 'Ruby.' And this time it seemed close by and I could feel a presence in the room. Then I saw a beautiful girl, who appeared to be between 23 and 25 years of age, standing beside me. She was wearing a long white dress and she smiled as she said, 'Ruby, come with me.' She said no more and then I knew I had left my body, and I followed her. I glanced back to see my body in the bed as we left the room and started down the street a half-block to State Street. When we arrived there the veil lifted and I knew I was in a different world—it all happened swifter than lightning—the change, I mean.

"I saw a meadow and lots of people. We went up some stairs, and I felt frightened suddenly and the young lady said to me, 'Be not afraid, I will always be with you.' She then took me further up the stairs, pausing to rest on the landing. I saw Orin Yancy, a recently deceased schoolmate of mine. I wished to speak to him but was told, 'No, you have not yet received the key or authority to go where you want to go.'

"We entered a building that had a large, very long hall, covered with tables at which people were sitting working or conversing. I looked as we passed to see if there was anyone I knew there. At one large table there were two empty chairs. Beside this table was a man who had laid hands on my head when I was doing baptisms for the dead. We passed on and found a place outside where we sat and talked. She told me that she was my guardian angel, and that she had been with me constantly since I came to earth. She instructed me about many other things, including the three degrees of glory. I felt that I should have lived a better life and accomplished more than I had; I voiced this to her and she said that I had nothing to fear, that I had lived well, but I had been a little inclined to judge people.

"As I saw others busy and happy, I felt that I wanted to go back and get my temple work done, so I could return and work in the celestial kingdom, so I knelt and prayed for another chance to return to earth. I prayed fervently with all my heart and soul for this petition to be granted. As I rose, I saw in the nearby area, the Savior with a group of people, he looked toward me and raised one of his arms toward me saying, 'You may go back and have the privilege of going through the temple. I have heard your prayers.'

"As we retraced our steps down the stairs I was aware of signs along the way which said, Judge Not That Ye Be Not Judged. We soon returned to my room and when I was once more in my body, I arose and checked the time—it was 9:30 a.m. I asked my sisters and later my parents why no one had awakened me. They all said they had forgotten.

"The above story does not include all the things I learned, things about the beauties of this life and the next; but I know that I will strive to live to return there, and strive to always say 'no' to all that is not pure and holy. This experience will always be a shining light in my life; much of it I cannot put in words."[4]

## A Guide Appears

At the time of death, a guide appears to accompany the newly deceased to the spirit world. The duty of an escort is to provide comfort and to ease the transition between mortality and the next life. Many times, the guide is a family member or a friend. Occasionally, the guide is someone specifically appointed to accompany spirits to the next sphere.[5]

### Woman Visits Spirit World

On February 17, 1867, an unnamed woman in her thirties left her body and was met by a female guide. The woman wrote about her experience as follows.

"I dreamed I was at home sick, and sitting in an arm chair, surrounded by my husband, mother, children, and friends. I was told, or rather felt, I was going to die; and after confiding the care of my children especially to my mother—she agreeing in accordance with my urgent solicitations to come and live with them—and bidding good-bye and pressing hands with those present, I felt sensibly the first approach of death, by a feeling of coldness and numbness commencing at my feet and thence to my body, until it reached the region of my heart: whereupon I became speechless, and felt as though I was approaching the unconscious state of sleep. My head involuntarily dropped back in the chair.

"At the return to consciousness, which was instantaneous, I found myself standing by the body from which I had just emerged, in a stooping posture, experiencing a sort of crampness in the breast and back, together with a feeling of general exhaustion. On looking up I discovered a female standing beside me in the attitude of one waiting, having her hand upon the chair, and attired in white flowing apparel. She at once introduced herself to me as my attendant, and invited me, when I was ready, to follow her. I inquired as to the cause of the peculiar feeling before referred to, and received in answer the following, which were her very words: 'Oh, every one feels that just after leaving the body, it is but momentary;' accompanied by a smile which indicated that she had often answered such questions before.

"While she was speaking I stood upright, and the feeling of crampness had already passed away. I then expressed a willingness to accompany her. She asked if I did not want to look at my body once more before leaving. I replied I did not, and felt an instinctive shudder at the thought of my body, and assured her I was but too glad to leave it. We then passed out at the door walking. I felt a delightful sense of lightness, as though I could raise myself from the ground by a simple effort of the will.

After proceeding through the gateway to the street, we glided somewhat rapidly along down the State road, southward, out of the city, until we reached a very large, round building, built entirely of white marble, supported by heavy white marble columns, and having but one entrance, which consisted simply of an opening between two of the columns, with a flight of steps leading to the interior. The marble of which this building was composed was not purely white, but had a yellow tinge, as though time-worn. On reaching the entrance, my companion informed me that I needed her attendance no longer. After directing me to ascend the steps and enter the building, my attendant turned and left me.

On entering the building I saw a man sitting nearly in the centre of the room at a large desk, directly under a peculiar canopy. Upon the desk was an exceedingly large book, having the appearance of a mammoth ledger. Four or five men were in a group near the desk, engaged in conversation with this personage, whom we will call the Director. I observed that the place had an air of business, and was free from ornament. . . .

"The Director looked towards me and said, 'Welcome, sister.' He was still engaged with those around him, all of whom were individuals whom I recognized as having seen before, but could not say when or where. They were dressed in the ordinary manner. . . . I had time to examine the interior of the hall, and discovered that the spaces between the columns—about twelve in all—were entirely open, so that I could see at once through and beyond them. Stationed at each of the pillars to the left, that separated these openings, were men who acted as guides.

"I ascertained this by seeing the Director point towards these men, and directing each of the men around him to go some to one man, some to another, and hearing him say, 'There is your guide—go there.'

"Through the first opening to my left were clouds of great density and blackness, the darkest I ever saw, and they seemed to be so near that they could be reached by the hand. The second opening to the left revealed dark threatening clouds, but not quite so black as the first. All the other openings to the left presented a dark atmosphere, thick and murky. . . .

"I turned to the right, where a far different picture met my gaze. Through all of these openings I saw the pure azure of heaven, clear and bright. Through the first space to my right I saw a city indescribably fair and beautiful, enveloped as it were in a thin mist of gold, and exquisitely beautiful; clouds of roseate hue were visible in the distance. The city was dotted with temples having lofty spires, and other buildings, combining in architectural designs more beauties than I had ever conceived it possible to exist, all of purest whiteness. Strains of lovely music floated on the atmosphere, that was more heavenly in its influence, and spoke more to the heart, than any music I had ever heard; it seem to come from a legion of musicians. . . .

"I was so enraptured by the sight of the city and the sound of the music, that for a time I was insensible of what was transpiring around me, from which I was aroused by the voice of the Director, saying, 'Sister, that is the Celestial City;' looking, as he spoke, toward the city I had seen. He then asked my name. . . . After glancing rapidly over the index, he at once turned to the latter end of the book, which, by its great weight, made a loud noise as it fell open on the desk.

"He read very rapidly what was on the open page before him, and while thus engaged, I stood trembling with anxiety, fearing I should not be assigned a place in the celestial city, although I had no apprehensions of being consigned to any of the dismal places to my left; but I felt as though I had not properly appreciated the blessings I had enjoyed, and remembered with astonishing vividness every time I had given expression to angry feelings and used improper words, every instance of my having corrected my children in anger; in a word, I recollected with great distinctness every folly and weakness of which I had been guilty since my marriage, a period of about ten years; but strange to say, nothing before that time.

"My anxiety was soon relieved by watching his countenance, which soon assumed a pleasant look. He rose and revealed a tall form, with a heavenly countenance abounding with masculine beauty. His eyes were grey, and beaming with expression. Taking me by the hand, he said, 'Sister, you are one of the privileged few who are to go to *that* celestial city,' (pointing to the city I had seen) and having read my thoughts, added, 'but you are not satisfied with yourself, are you?'

"I replied, 'No, sir, I am not.'

"He continued, "Shall I tell you one grand secret? 'Tis true you have not been wicked, but you have sometimes neglected your prayers, while in the body, and that gave the adversary strong hold over you; but our heavenly Father, when he sees his children err, is grieved—he is sad; but when he sees them show a spirit of repentance, and a desire to do right, he takes them under his protecting arm, he forgives, he forgets, he is full of mercy, he is full of charity; he is more merciful and charitable to us than we are to each other, and, with your children, is waiting anxiously to receive you.'

" 'Oh, then,' I exclaimed in an ecstasy of delight, 'let me go to my children!'

" 'Not yet,' said he, 'not yet; you cannot leave the earth until your body is buried; take my advice and return to your home, for it is not long you will remain, and, moreover, before you can go to the celestial city, you must go into that room (pointing to the door) and change your dress.'

"Then for the first time I looked to see how I was attired. I ascertained I had on a robe of exquisite whiteness. I remembered that during my illness I wore earrings, and felt my ears to find out if I had them still, but I had not. I then examined my dress carefully to see if there were any pins, hooks and eyes, or buttons about it, but found none of those things, strings being used instead.

"My hair next drew my attention. I found it free from hair pins, combs or net of any kind; but instead of hanging loosely on my shoulders, the ends were nicely curled under in waves, and it was glossy and soft as the finest silk. I then looked at my hands and found them almost transparent, having a pink look similar to the natural hand when held between the eyes and a strong light; and yet my sense of touch seemed as real as ever. On the whole I was extremely gratified with my appearance, and thought it could not be improved.

"The Director again reading my thoughts, told me that when I entered that room I should exchange my robe for one of *dazzling* whiteness, before leaving for the celestial city, and added, 'You cannot come here then. . . .'

"I then departed from the hall and glided with increased rapidity through this city to my home therein. On entering the parlor, I saw an assemblage of relatives and friends, who were listening to the funeral ceremony which had been going on for some time. . . . On gazing upon what had been once myself, I again instinctively shuddered at the sight, and felt a sensation of loathing come upon me, and felt deeply grateful that I had escaped from its cold, clayey [sic] prison house. My husband was sitting with his head downward, and resting on one hand, apparently absorbed in thought. My mother was almost overcome with grief. My children were also present, but, strange to say, I felt no particular anxiety about them, feeling doubly assured that they would be well taken care of and grateful to find that my mother had remembered her promise.

"President Brigham Young was preaching the funeral sermon. I heard him say I was far happier than those who were left, and that there was no cause for regretting my death. I thought I would have given anything if I could have only told them how happy I felt; and earnestly did I desire to communicate something that would stimulate them to increased diligence and faithfulness, but I had not the power to do so."

She then decided to visit some of the familiar places she knew on earth. As she walked along, she said it was easy to distinguish which were mortals and which were spirits and added, "There was all the variety of age, rank, dress, manner, speed in walking, &c, as seen ordinarily."

Then she went back to the marble building and saw the same personage at the desk. She said several wicked-looking men were standing nearby, waiting to receive word on where they would go.

"They seemed noisy, and even boisterous, talking among themselves but when the Director addressed them with these solemn words, "There is your guide, go there,' and pointed to the gloomy opening at the left, feelings of unutterable anguish came over them . . . that of absolute despair. . . . They moaned, wailed piteously and some gnashed their teeth and smote their breasts. The spectacle was too appalling; I had to turn away or my feelings would have overcome me.

"Immediately my gaze met the piercing eye of the Director, looking sternly at me. He said, 'Sympathise *not* with them; their paths were plain before them, but they chose the evil and refused the good, not with their eyes closed, but with eyes wide open; and they must suffer the consequence.' For a moment I stood lost in thought, and said to myself, 'How few there are who *go to the right!*'

" 'Yes,' responded the Director, 'few indeed;' and then added, his countenance lighting up with a beaming smile, 'I suppose you are now ready to go to the Celestial City.' I replied I was anxious to go there."

She then looked through the opening and saw the city and heard heavenly music. Hearing footsteps, she turned and saw a man she recognized. Without being told, she knew he would be going to the celestial city after his body was buried. She went to the threshold, but before she could step over it and into the celestial city, she suddenly came back to her mortal body.

"At this moment I awoke and found it was the break of day. I felt very much exhausted. I remained in bed two or three hours in order to gain strength; when I arose I trembled with weakness, so that it was with difficulty I succeeded in getting down stairs; and during the whole day I felt as though I had but just recovered from a severe illness."[6]

## *Lorena Larsen*

Lorena Larsen was guided to the spirit world by a former bishop, Dennison L. Harris.

"After the year of 1900, one day I lay down on my bed and took a nap, and while sleeping I thought I passed out of my body, and that Dennison L. Harris, former bishop [and grandfather of

President Harris of BYU] was there and said he had been sent to escort me to the place where I was to go. I pled with him not to take me, but let me go back into my body and stay with my children until they were all grown, married, and could take care of themselves. He said the Lord had decided I should come.

"As we traveled along the road, I found how valuable the Temple ordinances were, as we met the guards along the way. I still pled with him to let me go back, and he told me that we would pass by the mansion where the Lord lived, and there was no chance for me to go back unless the Lord changed the decision.

"Presently we came to the Lord's mansion and were almost in sight of the city where we were to go, when I told him to please go in and tell the Lord if he would only let me go back that I would endure everything which came to me of trials.

"He went into the building and I heard him tell the Lord all that I had said. The Lord said, 'If she goes now her salvation is sure, but if she goes back she will have to take chances.' And as I stood there and heard their conversation I could see that there were trials and obstacles for me in the future. Brother Harris came and repeated all that had been said, and I told him I would go back and take chances. We then returned on the same path on which we came.

"I thought it was an awful ordeal to re-enter the body, the feeling was like one's limbs going to sleep, as we call it, only intensified a hundred times. And when I awoke my face and head, even my nose, had that awful feeling in them. I arose, then knelt and thanked the Lord for life and health, and for my family, and the many blessings I had received from Him from my earliest recollection."[7]

## Notes

1.  *Teachings of Presidents of the Church: Joseph F. Smith* (Salt Lake City: The Church of Jesus Christ of Latter-day Saints, 1998), 88.

2.  Brigham Young, *Discourses of Brigham Young,* comp. and ed. John A. Widstoe (Salt Lake City: Deseret Book, 1961), 368–9.

3.  Marlene Bateman Sullivan, *Gaze into Heaven: Near-death Experiences in Early Church History,* (Springville; Cedar Fort Inc.), 11–12.

4.  Norma Clark Larsen, *His Everlasting Love,* (Bountiful: Horizon Publishers, 1977), 136-38. Used with permission of Horizon Publishers & Distributors.

5.  Marlene Bateman Sullivan, *Gaze into Heaven: Near-death Experiences in Early Church History,* (Springville: Cedar Fort Inc., 2013), 19–20.

6.  *The Latter-day Saints' Millennial Star* vol. 29 no. 24 (1867), 369–74. Also, *Deseret News* 27 March, 1867, 98.

7.  Floy Isabell Larsen Turner, *Lorena Eugenia Washburn Larsen, A Mother in Israel,* (Courtesy of the Church History Library, The Church of Jesus Christ of Latter-day Saints).

*Chapter Three*

# Arrival in the Spirit World

ALTHOUGH DEATH SEPARATES us from our body, we will continue to be the same in character and personality as we were in mortality. Daniel Ludlow, a professor of religion who taught at Brigham Young University, said, "The spirit continues to exist as real and as lively after its separation from the physical body as it did before. The term death essentially has to do with separation. Thus at the time of our temporal-physical death, the spirit body is separated from the physical body and from the physical world it has known while in the physical body."[1]

There will be no changes in our character after we die. We will be the same person in the next life as we are now, taking with us the same dispositions and tendencies we developed while on earth. David O. McKay stated, "I believe with all my soul in the persistence of personality after death. I cannot believe otherwise. Even reason and observation demonstrate that to me. . . . Personality is persistent, and that is the message of comfort. . . . Death cannot touch the spirit of man."[2]

Heber C. Kimball also taught that our personalities and temperament will remain intact: "Have I not told you often that the separation of body and spirit makes no difference in the moral and intellectual condition of the spirit? When a person, who has always been good and faithful to his God, lays down his body in the dust, his spirit will remain the same in the spirit world. It is not the body that has control over the spirit, as to its disposition, but it is the spirit that controls the body."[3]

In the Book of Mormon, the prophet Alma declares that the spirit will have the same tendencies to religious beliefs and personal righteousness—or the lack of it—that he had while living in mortality. "That same spirit which doth possess your bodies at the time that ye go out of this life, that same spirit will have power to possess your body in that eternal world" (Alma 34:34).

The spirit world is much like life on earth. A number of people who visited the spirit world remarked that life there felt as real as though they were still on earth. There was nothing strange or peculiar about their surroundings, and they had no feeling of unreality. Visitors said that the people they met in the spirit world seemed natural.

Brigham Young taught, "When you are in the spirit world, everything there will appear as natural as things now do. Spirits will be familiar with spirits in the spirit world—will converse, behold, and exercise every variety of communication one with another as familiarly and naturally as while here in tabernacles. There, as here, all things will be natural, and you will understand them as you now understand natural things."[4]

## Charles V. Anderson

Charles V. Anderson visited the spirit world shortly before he became ill. He said his visit was very real and declared it was not a dream. Charles believed his experience was given to prepare him to endure a serious illness that befell him afterwards. Charles wrote about his visit in a letter dated February 29, 1932.

"The following is what I experienced just prior to my illness, which began in the latter part of January, and lasted through

February. I stood at the portals of the great Beyond and looked in. I did not see any magnificent mansions, nor did I see a soul or any form of animal life, but I beheld a flower garden so wonderfully beautiful that no human tongue however eloquent, or pen however masterly, could even begin to describe it. The flowers were of the same kind I had seen before, but much larger. The coloring was very clear and distinct, and wonderfully harmonious.

"It must have been morning, for the dew was yet on the flowers, and there was a life-stirring influence emerging from them that thrilled my very soul. I wish I could describe the light that shone upon the scene. It was more brilliant than sunlight, yet not so dazzling, and it felt so life-giving, soothing and peaceful—like a smile from heaven above.

"The scene occupied the whole opposite wall of the room and was divided into three groups, one in the center and one on each side. The path that lead [led] around the center group and towards the back was of a medium tan color, but was not made of cement, nor was it gravel, and was very even and well-kept. An indescribable happiness filled my whole being, and I was overcome by a desire to step in to the beautiful garden, for it seemed to require only one step, as there was no fence or gate and my feet almost touched the pathway, when I heard a man's voice gently saying: 'Not yet, not yet, you have more to do.'

"The scene ended. It can not be said that it was the hallucinations of a fever-racked brain, for I had not yet taken ill. It was two days before [I became ill] and I felt perfectly well. The scene, or vision, did not last more than a minute and a half, and I was fully awake. I had just closed my eyes preparatory to sleep when the scene appeared immediately.

"I did not sleep until a long time after; I was so full of happy and peaceful thoughts. I knew I would have to pass through a severe sickness, even close to death, but I did not feel the least alarmed, for I knew I would pull through. This was not a dream; it was actual; it was real; I saw and felt it; and the scene is just as vivid to my vision this minute, as it was when I beheld it. If I ever had any fear of death, it has entirely passed away, for now I know and understand."[5]

## Clothing

Many of those who visited the spirit world mention seeing people dressed in white clothing. In the New Testament, John the Revelator speaks of seeing spirits clad in white robes. "I saw under the altar the souls of them that were slain for the word of God, and for the testimony which they held. . . . And white robes were given unto every one of them; and it was said unto them, that they should rest yet for a little season" (Revelation 6:9, 11).

When the Savior appeared to the Nephites, He wore a white robe. "As they understood they cast their eyes up again towards heaven; and behold, they saw a Man descending out of heaven; and he was clothed in a white robe" (3 Nephi 11:8).

Joseph Smith said that when the angel Moroni appeared to him, "he had on a loose robe of most exquisite whiteness. It was a whiteness beyond anything earthly I had ever seen; nor do I believe that any earthly thing could be made to appear so exceedingly white and brilliant" (Joseph Smith—History 1:31).

Although white clothing seems to be the norm, a few visitors saw spirits dressed in street clothes or wearing dark or light-colored clothing. In his experience, Heber Q. Hale saw soldiers wearing uniforms (see chapter 8).

A few early-day Latter-day Saints who had near-death experiences saw people dressed in other types of clothing, such as Ella Jensen, who saw her uncle dressed as if he had gone fishing—which is what he was doing when he drowned.[6]

## David O. McKay

In May of 1921, President David O. McKay was traveling by boat to Apia, Samoa, when he saw into the spirit world and saw people dressed in flowing white robes.

"We sailed all day on the smoothest sea of our entire trip. . . . Nearing Savaii, we could see with the aid of our field glasses the 'Spouting Horns,' which looked like geysers. On our right we caught a glimpse of the little village nestling safely in the mouth of an extinct volcano on the little island of Apolima.

"Toward evening, the reflection of the afterglow of a beautiful sunset was most splendid. The sky was tinged with pink, and the clouds lingering around the horizon were fringed with various hues of crimson and orange. . . . Gradually, the shadows became deeper and heavier, and then all merged into a beautiful calm twilight that made the sea look like a great mirror upon which fell the faint light of the crescent moon.

"Pondering still upon this beautiful scene, I lay in my berth at ten o'clock that night and thought to myself: Charming as it is, it doesn't stir my soul with emotion as do the innocent lives of children, and the sublime characters of loved ones and friends. . . .

"I then fell asleep, and beheld in vision something infinitely sublime. In the distance I beheld a beautiful white city. Though it was far away, yet I seemed to realize that all trees [were covered] with luscious fruit, shrubbery with gorgeously tinted leaves, and flowers in perfect bloom abounded everywhere.

"The clear sky above seemed to reflect these beautiful shades of color. I then saw a great concourse of people approaching the city. Each one wore a white flowing robe and a white headdress. Instantly my attention seemed centered upon their leader, and though I could see only the profile of his features and his body, I recognized him at once as my Savior! The tint and radiance of his countenance were glorious to behold. There was a peace about him which seemed sublime—it was divine!

"The city, I understood, was his. It was the City Eternal; and the people following him were to abide there in peace and eternal happiness. But who were they?

"As if the Savior read my thoughts, he answered by pointing to a semicircle that then appeared above them, and on which were written in gold the words:

"These Are They Who Have Overcome the World—

"Who Have Truly Been Born Again!

"When I awoke, it was breaking day over Apia harbor."[7]

## *William Butler*

During his experience, William Butler saw many Church leaders dressed in white.

"I saw a beautiful building on the shore. . . . Brigham Young and Heber C. Kimball were the first men I saw. –they reached out their hands and helped me into the building. –when I got inside, the first men I saw were Joseph and Hyrum Smith, the prophet and patriarch drest [*sic*] in white, and the twelve Apostles also drest in white. –to the best of my knowledge I believed them to be the twelve spoken of in the Book of mormon. [Th]ey sat alone at a table on the South side of a room. . . .–each on[e] . . . were writing. . . .—to the best of my opinion, they were interceding for the dead.

"I went to the far end of the room, and returned (seeing them all busy at work.) and came to Joseph and Hyrum, who were conversing with Brigham and Heber—Brigham and Heber stood up whilst Joseph and Hyrum sat down –I stood and gazed on Joseph and Hyrum. –particularly on Joseph. –Joseph reached out his hand to me, and said, 'this is bone and sinew. –be not afraid.'

"his countenance and the appearance of his flesh, was very bright and dazzling [to] behold, in fact this was the appearance of all the resurrected ones. –Joseph then told me pointing to Brigham (and after he had shook hands with me) and Heber. –these are the men to follow."[8]

# Notes

1.  Daniel Hansen Ludlow, *The Post-earthly Spiritual Existence*, (Courtesy of the Church History Library, The Church of Jesus Christ of Latter-day Saints).

2.  David O McKay, *Gospel Ideals, Selections from the Discourses of David O. McKay*, (Salt Lake City: Improvement Era Publication, 1953), 54–55.

3.  Heber C Kimball, *Journal of Discourses*, vol. 3 (London: Latter-day Saints' Book Depot, 1856), 108.

4.  Brigham Young, *Journal of Discourses*, vol. 7 (London: Latter-day Saints' Book Depot, 1860), 239.

5.  Charles V. Anderson, *Faith-promoting Collection 1882-1974*, box 1, folder 3, (Courtesy of the Church History Library, The Church of Jesus Christ of Latter-day Saints).

6.  Marlene Bateman Sullivan, *Gaze into Heaven: Near-death Experiences in Early Church History*, (Springville: Cedar Fort Inc., 2013), 171.

7.  David O. McKay, *Cherished Experiences from the Writings of President David O. McKay*, comp. Clare Middlemiss (Salt Lake City: Deseret Book, 1976), 59–60.

8.  William Butler, *Autobiography 1850–1875*, (Courtesy of the Church History Library, The Church of Jesus Christ of Latter-day Saints).

*Chapter Four*

# The Spirit Body

OUR SPIRITS LOOK like our physical bodies. While speaking at general conference, Apostle Erastus Snow mentioned this, saying, "Now what is this spirit? It is a being precisely as we are seen here to-day; and if you ask, 'How does brother Snow's spirit look when it is disembodied?' Why, you just look at me now, and you can answer the question. How does the spirit of my wife look? Why, just look at her and see. . . . We are the same beings . . . the same features exactly."[1]

Although our spirit bodies will be identical to our physical bodies, they will be free from any earthly ailments and disabilities that afflicted us while on earth. Orson Pratt declared, "We, as Latter-day Saints, believe that the spirits that occupy these tabernacles have form and likeness similar to the human tabernacle. Of course there may be deformities existing in connection with the outward tabernacle which do not exist in connection with the spirit that inhabits it. These tabernacles become deformed by accident in various ways, sometimes at birth, but this may not altogether or in any degree deform the spirits that dwell within them."[2]

It appears that the powers and capabilities of the spirit body will surpass those of the physical body in regards to vision, communication, movement, and comprehension. In addition, our capacity to remember will be increased. Joseph F. Smith said, "May I say to you that in reality a man cannot forget anything? He may have a lapse of memory; he may not be able to recall at the moment a thing that he knows, or words that he has spoken; he may not have the power at his will to call up these events and words; but let God Almighty touch the mainspring of the memory, and awaken recollection, and you will find then that you have not even forgotten a single idle word that you have spoken."[3]

## Vision Is Magnified

When our spirit leaves our body, our vision will be greatly enhanced and we will be able to see vast distances. While Heber C. Kimball was in England on a mission, he had a vision and found his eyesight was significantly improved. Heber said the reason he could see so well was because he was seeing with his spiritual eyes. "All at once my vision was opened, and the walls of the building were no obstruction to my seeing, for I saw nothing but the visions that presented themselves. Why did not the walls obstruct my view? Because my spirit could look through the walls of that house, for I looked with that spirit, element, and power, with which angels look; and as God sees all things."[4]

### Philip Haskins

When Philip Haskins visited the spirit world in 1798, his eyesight was strengthened beyond description and he could see through the regions of space. Phillip writes:

"I was born in the town of Taunton . . . State of Massachusetts; . . . I followed farming until I arrived at the age of eighteen, I then took to the seas and followed them for seven years, chiefly whaling. I then returned to Berkley and was married to Mary Mirric . . . by her I had eight children. . . .

"Soon after I was married, these words came to my mind with great power, 'turn ye, turn ye for why will ye die, oh house of Israel.' These words followed me from day to day I knew not that they were in the bible; but on searching it I found them."

A year later, Philip and his wife were living with a family who invited them to be baptized into their religion. Phillip declined, but one morning he was lying in bed when the following words were impressed onto his mind:

"Arise and be baptized, calling on the name of the Lord &c."

"I accordingly arose and made my desires known to the brethren; it being in the month of January, they cut a hole in the ice and I was baptized by Elder Hyme, and joined the church and lived happy in Christ for several years.

"During this time my mother died; she had never made an open profession of religion and it labored hard in my mind, what had become of her. These thoughts kept impressed in my mind, what has become of her—where has she gone; these words seemed impressed in my mind, and the more I tho't of it the more anxious I felt to know her condition. . . . One night as I lay in bed with my wife, what time in the night this view happened I cannot tell; the first I knew I was almost to the chamber floor with a holy angel, who had come to be my guide to the mansions of eternal day; the room was as light as day, and my guide turned me round and I saw my body lying in bed with my wife apparently asleep. I likewise saw my children sleeping in their bed; I next found myself in open air.

"I had all my rational powers of mind. My eye-sight was strengthened beyond description. I was carried I cannot tell how far or how swift, at length through the regions of space my eyes caught sight of eternal day, or what is called heaven. I saw my mother seated on the right hand of Christ; she then appeared to be millions of miles distant, but the light of eternal day was so bright and my eye-sight so clear and piercing that I saw and knew her in a moment. While I stood viewing and admiring this shining abode with the deepest wonder and admiration these words came into my mind. Rev. 21–22–23—while I was viewing my mother at this amazing distance, it seemed but a moment and I was there.

"On going up to her she thus addressed me. 'Well Philip, you have soon came after your mother.'

"I replied, 'Yes mother. I have soon followed you.'

"There appeared to be a girdle around her waist which was of the purest gold, and on it was reading, the letters of which were smaller than the eye of a cambric needle;

"She said, 'Come Philip, read what is round my waist.'

"I replied, 'I will mother if I can.'

"I then began and read one verse, upon which the heavenly angels struck in and sung the same; I then proceeded to read another verse, which was sung likewise, and so on until the whole was finished. I then looked round on the angels and those just ones made perfect, but in attempting to describe their glory, their powers and loveliness, language fails me, for no tongue can express, no heart conceive nor understanding comprehend the thousandth part of their happy, holy and heavenly appearances.

"Their skin appeared like that of an infant, or a child eight or nine months old. There was one that stood close by me, and whom I viewed to my satisfaction—he like the rest appeared to be three or four feet above the streets which were of the purest gold. They were larger than a common sized man . . . They had on robes of the most beautiful white that my eyes ever saw, but their glorious features cannot be described; their glorious features and their immortal music was such, that no mortal could endure it unless strengthen with immortal powers and faculties to see and know people for millions of miles. . . .

"The reader may think it strange that I should know people here which I never before saw, but I most certainly did, I knew Christ. I saw some of the Apostles, which I instantly knew; I also saw several of my old acquaintance. I moved on a little further and saw one Nathaniel McCumber, with whom I was well acquainted: we shook hands, I asked him how long he had been in this knew abode, he replied about twenty days, and how long said he have you been here? I have just come I repeated. At this we passed on; I saw one of my ship-mates and would have spoke to him, but my guide would not admit it; so we passed on and joined with Peter and John, two of Christ's beloved disciples. Peter was the largest and John was the slimmest and handsomest.

"I had no thoughts of ever returning to this earthly habitation again, but to my great disappointment I understood by my guide that I must return. It appeared to be an immence distance to this earth, and the next that I knew, my spirit was returning to my body again and the daylight shined into the windows.

"How long I had been gone I could not tell, I was in great distress when my blood began to circulate, it first began at my heart, and from thence extended in to all my members; I tried to move but I could not; I tried to speak but I could not; at length my blood having reached and circulated in all my limbs, I found I could move; I then awoke my wife and related the occurrence, but she treated it all as a dream and said if what I had said was a reality, and if I had actually been there, I could remember the verses that was on the golden girdle. I told her I could and likewise rehersed them to her, which soon convinced her of the reality of it. They were then taken from my memory and I could never remember them more, for they were the language of immortals and not to be retained by mortals.

"I now felt more happy in the love of Christ than ever. . . . I believed as little in dreams, visions, or revelations in our day, perhaps, as any one, but this I certainly know, that my soul left its earthly habitation and was guided by a heavenly messenger to the regions of eternal day."

Although Philip basked in the peace and joy that came from this miraculous experience, his feelings did not last. He wrote,

"Thus I lived happy in the Lord for several years, but at length I was overtaken with anger, and I gave way to it till it became so headstrong that I became its slave. I fell from my stedfastness—I grieved the spirit of God, and lost that sweet peace out of my soul, and now I feel the gnawing of that worm, that never dies, and the fire that is never quenched."

The account states that Philip Haskins died in black despair in 1820, twenty years after his visit to the spirit world.[5]

## Communication Is Different

We will be able to communicate perfectly in the spirit world, without the struggles we sometimes face now to put our thoughts into words. A number of people who visited the spirit world indicated that speech was not needed because spirits were able to discern one another's thoughts. While this method appeared to be the most common method of communication, spirits are also able to speak to one another.

The Lord revealed to Joseph Smith that God communicates with mortals through their hearts and minds. "Yea, behold, I will tell you in your mind and in your heart, by the Holy Ghost, which shall come upon you" (D&C 8:2). Apparently this divine means of communication will be expanded in the next life.

Elder Orson Pratt said, "How do you suppose that spirits after they leave these bodies, communicate one with another? Do they communicate their ideas by the actual vibrations of the atmosphere [speech] the same as we do? I think not. I think if we could be made acquainted with the kind of language by which spirits converse with spirits, we would find that they . . . have undoubtedly a more refined system among them of communicating their ideas. . . . For instance, the Book of Mormon tells us, that the angels speak by the power of the Holy Ghost, and man when under the influence of it, speaks the language of angels. Why does he speak in this language? Because the Holy Ghost suggests the ideas which he speaks; and it gives him utterance to convey them to the people. . . . Suppose, instead of having arbitrary sounds, such as we have here, to communicate these ideas, that the Holy Ghost itself, through a certain process and power should enable him to unfold that knowledge to another spirit, all in an instant."[6]

## Florence Forrest

Florence Forrest was born in Nova Scotia in 1888 and converted to the gospel in 1921. As an adult, her health was not good, and Florence was hospitalized a number of times. In May of 1909, Florence went to Hyde Park General Hospital for an operation and while there visited the spirit world. Florence commented that in the spirit world, people's manner of speaking was different than what she was used to. Florence recounted the tale of after she was put to sleep for her operation:

"The next thing I knew I realized I was nearing an entrance, and just then saw two hands open a gate, and saw the back of a person walking away. I knew it was Christ, the Lord, and said to myself 'My Lord, he has opened the gate of Heaven, for me to come in.' I saw he wore a long robe, the purest white I had ever seen. His hair was also white, so white, that the word white cannot explain what it was like. He went quickly out of sight.

"I stepped inside. How happy I was, that instant that I was free from body, everything that had been holding me back all my life. I then looked around and attempted to go on but something stopped me, I did not know what. The most gloriously lighted place was before me. The most glorious light shone over me, which gave me clear understanding.

"Beside me was my infant baby I had lost two years before. It knew me and appeared much older and to understand things, but was gone in an instant. My earthly father came running towards me. He looked so happy and pleased to see me and was about to kiss me but was stopped. He looked out over this earth, which seemed to be such a little way from us. As he turned to go away I saw he walked as though his body was not solid and strong as the Lord's was when I saw him walking away.

"In the midst of this place, was what we here would call a desk. It was not called that there. Words there, or the manner of speaking was not the same as here. It seemed as though someone was behind that desk though I did not see anyone. I was still near the entrance and although I did not see him, I felt the Lord was speaking.

"I was asked if I wanted to come in and was told if I entered I must stay. I could do as I wished. I wanted to enter but then thought of my baby on earth who was one year old. I looked right back and saw him and then said 'I would rather go back and bring up my baby, for there is no one else to bring him up as I was brought up.'

"I saw him outside the door on the ground playing with little stones and I thought his father should watch him; he might put a stone in his mouth. Then I turned and I said, 'My Lord, my Lord, is this Heaven? If I had entered would I have come in here?'

"He said, 'This is not Heaven. Here is where you would learn of me. Here is where you would become perfect as your Father in Heaven is perfect.' He then talked with me and said many things that I cannot repeat.

"I saw what looked like a heavy roll of something solid that could not be moved. I asked what it was. I was told laws of God are measured there and cannot be broken. One end began at the gate of where I went in and it extended inside a distance. I thought to myself, how strong that is, how did I get past it.

"I looked up and asked, 'If my husband died would he come in here? He is not a member of any church, but reads the Bible a great deal.'

"I was told: 'Leave your husband alone. He is all right. The churches are not right; they are all wrong.'

"He said I was faithful in the beginning and I asked what he meant. He did not answer me on this. He praised me for wanting to stay back and bring my child up. He said he would bless him [her child] with wisdom and understanding beyond his age. He would bless him with strength to overcome evil and temptations in this life. . . .

"I asked if I would be well after this operation and he told me no. I must trust him and look to him for my health. I then said I would like to have more children. He said I was not strong in the beginning and I need not have more children.

"I asked, 'If I were not in the right church, what church should I join?'

"He said, 'None of them.'

"I asked what I should do. He said to be patient, in his own due time it would come to me.

"I said, 'We have the Bible and read it.'

"He said, 'The Bible is not all.'

"I then saw two hands open up the desk, which was also pure white. It was glorious white from the light constantly shining on it, and I raised myself on my toes to see inside. I saw two hands lay out a lot of books and it seemed I knew them all. I talked to him about them, and he said I needed to have them all. I tried to reach them, but could not. I saw what I now know was the Book of Mormon. I saw the Doctrine and Covenants. It seemed the Doctrine and Covenants book had been mine before, but that I had forgotten about it. How happy, how thrilled I was to see it again. I was told I could not take them then but if I kept faithful and would accept them, they would be brought to me. . . .

"We talked again about my husband and me and about our marriage. He told me we were not married. He told me if my husband and I came in there then together we would not be as husband and wife. He told me I must be married in his temple, and just then a beautiful building was shown to me. I just gazed upon it and thought how beautiful it was and wondered what it was made of and how I wanted to go into it. In an instant it seemed I stood beside it and placed my hand against one side of it.

"I said, 'why it's built of stone.' I looked it over and saw how beautifully it was curved and how it did shine under the light. One end looked to be build up higher than the other and the light shone more brilliantly on this higher part than on the other.

"I asked, 'Why is that part of the temple so much brighter than the other.'

"I was answered that God visits his people in that part of the temple. I noticed the other part was not so bright and was told that this part was for man.

"I then came back to where I had before stood but thought nothing of how I came there. The one in whose presence I stood told me that if I accepted all this and remained faithful as I was in the beginning, great blessings that had been promised me would be mine. I would bear children and it would be a great blessing to my dear ones, it was promised to me as my portion in the beginning. . . He told me that people had all gone wrong. They are no more humble to accept him as He is. He said they do not please God in the way they are living. He told me He was Jesus Christ, my Lord, and all things were done through him. He told me my prayers should be said through him to God in Heaven. He said in his own due time they are answered.

"I said how happy I was to hear things. . . . . I then looked around and saw a man standing on what seemed like the edge of the place where I was. How I looked at him for he appeared so outstanding. He had a solid body, just like our own. His feet, it seemed, were not touching anything and I think they were bare. He wore a long white robe. I noticed how rich and attractive it looked, as it hung down over his shoulders and arm. His hair was black and came down to the neck. His right arm was raised and pointed out over the earth where he was looking.

"I noticed how near it seemed to the earth. I asked what he was doing and was told he was pleading with the people on earth to come back to the temple of God but they would not. They were all going their way.

"I was permitted to go and looked down over the earth. I was amazed to see how close this wonderful place is to the earth, and I saw that this beautiful light where I was could not shine down on the earth. How badly I felt that people had all turned their backs on God. I did not know before that people were all going so wrong.

"Then I turned myself about and was shown a dark and most horrible looking place. I was told it was Hell. It was not black darkness, but was just an awful darkness with no light. There appeared to be no bottom of it and [it] was horribly big; many people were there, trying to get through it. It looked as if they were wallowing through something that was holding them down. It was so big and dark and awful that it was not possible to see how to get through. I then noticed that some were getting out, somehow but I could not be sure how. . . .

"When I awakened, I was told I have been gone or unconscious since ten o'clock in the morning and it was then 4:30 in the afternoon. . . . The first thing I thought was how dark and dismal this world seemed and I wished I had stayed and not came back. Everything seemed so gloomy to me. . . . Finally I was able to go home and gradually recovered. . . .

"Eleven years later a Mormon elder came to my door and I told him I would go to one of his meetings. . . . At the time I regarded it no differently than any other. . . . After the service, Elder Baker held up the '*Voice of Warning*.' and I saw the person on it that I had seen in my experience as I lay in the hospital years before. For a moment I almost fainted and I had to sit down, I felt so weak. When I got up I asked him if he could tell me who that was.

"He told me that it was a heavenly messenger whom we believe has spoken again to the earth in our day. . . Then I saw and recognized the Book of Mormon, the Doctrine and Covenants and other books, and I asked if I could borrow them to read. . . . Some time later I received some pamphlets from Elder Mark E. Peterson with the picture of the Salt Lake Temple on them and I recognized that building at once. I had seen it in my 'dream.' I can never tell anyone how happy this made me feel, how glad and satisfied I was that I had now found what I have been waiting for so many years. . . .

"My husband also was very happy about this for I had told him all about it. He had never been interested in any church but seemed all ready to accept the teachings the same as I. . . .

"I cannot find words to express how without any doubts whatsoever I know I belong to the only true Church of God. I've wished many times that others could see what I have seen. . . . Anyone who will accept the teachings of this Church and live them will never regret it. I say this with all my soul, in the name of Jesus Christ. Amen. Sister Florence Forrest."[7]

## Spirits Can Move About Easily

Once the spirit is freed from its physical body, it is capable of moving quickly and easily and can travel great distances at enormous speeds. This happens because once the spirit is separated from the physical body, it will not be bound by physical laws but by spiritual laws. Brigham Young stated, "As quickly as the spirit is unlocked from this house of clay, it is free to travel with lightning speed to any planet, or fixed star, or to the uttermost part of the earth, or to the depths of the sea, according to the will of Him who dictates."[8] He also said, "[Spirits] move with ease and like lightning. If we want to visit Jerusalem, or this, that, or the other place—and I presume we will be permitted if we desire—there we are, looking at its streets."[9]

Archie Graham, who visited the spirit world during a near-death experience, said, "My body was light in weight. I could move about with the least exertion. . . . I felt as though I could fly I was so light."[10]

Part of the reason spirits have increased capabilities is because spirit bodies are composed of different matter than our physical bodies. Joseph Smith said, "The spirit is a substance; that it is material, but that it is more pure, elastic and refined matter than the body; that it existed before the body, can exist in the body; and will exist separate from the body."[11]

## George D. Hughes

George D. Hughes said that he and his guide traveled through the air at a tremendous speed and that once his visit was over, their trip back to mortality only a matter of seconds.

George D. Hughes was born in Spanish Fork, Utah, in 1898. In April of 1917, George enlisted in the Marine Corps and was sent overseas to help stop the German army from invading Paris. In July of 1918, George was returning from a reconnaissance mission when he became tired. Spotting an empty foxhole, he crawled into it and fell asleep.

When he woke, George found himself in a spacious room. It was well lit, although he couldn't see any lamp or light fixture. When a man in white approached him, George said, "I presume I'm in the spirit world."

The man told George he was correct and handed him white clothing. Before changing, George asked, "Can you give me permission to go back?"

"No, I cannot."

"Then take me to someone who can."

"They left the original building together and came out on a park, a breathtaking spot with lawns, trees, bushes, and flowers. They walked along the edge of the park, passing buildings on the right with the park on their left. Other individuals crossed the park diagonally, following a smaller footpath. . . . Following his guide's lead, he entered a second building where three men sat around a large, beautiful table. George spoke to the personage in the center and pleaded to be allowed to return.

"The man said, 'You surely couldn't want to go back—not to that place of war and dirt?'"

They talked on, and George asked him how he came to be in the spirit world, saying, "I don't know how this happened. The last thing I remember was lying down to go to sleep."

The middle personage explained that a bomb had exploded over his foxhole, killing him and many other young men who were nearby. George again asked to return to earth. Even though the spirit world was lovely, he knew he needed to return. The man said they would consider George's request and, in the meantime, had George's guide show him around.

One thing George noticed was that everyone spoke the same language, and he understood it, even though he didn't remember hearing it spoken before.

When they returned, the middle personage told George he could return. He and his guide left, and suddenly they were traveling through the air at a tremendous speed. The trip took only a few seconds.

When they came close to the battlefield, the guide pointed and said, "There's your shell hole."

There was a jagged hole eight to ten yards in diameter. Twenty bodies lay around it wrapped in sheets or blankets as a group of workers hurried to transport the bodies. A doctor used his stethoscope to listen for heartbeats, but in every case he wrote on a dated tag, "Death Confirmed."

When the blanket over one body was pulled away, George stared in shock. "Hey, that's me!"

He saw the doctor write on his tag, "Death Confirmed," and watched an orderly rewrap his body. The bodies were then placed in a mass grave. (Later the dead were dug up and reburied in solitary plots or shipped home to relatives.) George saw with horror that dirt was being shoveled on top of his body. His guide urged him to hurry.

George did not remember how he reentered his body, but he found himself inside a blanket that had been tied at both ends. Feeling the thud of dirt falling on him, George wriggled and pulled his feet up, bending his knees. One of the men noticed his movements and pawed the dirt away. Others joined in. They unwrapped his blanket and pulled him out. George looked at his tag and saw his death was confirmed July 22, which meant his spirit had been separated from his body for three days, since the last he remembered it was July 19. An ambulance rushed George to the hospital, where he spent some time recovering before being sent to Virginia for additional medical treatment.[12]

## Jane Cish

Jane Cish was a teenager in 1780 when she left her body and followed her guide to the spirit world. Jane said that nothing hindered their movement through vast regions of space. She writes:

"Finding myself indisposed, I withdrew to my chamber, laid me down on the bed, and said—Lord, let thy hand support a feeble wretch; If I have deceived myself, let me know it; or if thou hast any good in store for me let me now find it. I scarce had done speaking, when I found myself seized with a kind of an easy, sleeping, fainting fit; and found my senses to alter and decline.

"I soon found myself disengaged from my body, and my senses amazingly enlarged. I began to view this new scene with wonder, when one in white, whose brightness enlightened the room, said to me, 'Follow me.'

"He ascended, I ascended after; and there seemed to be nothing that obstructed either our sight or motion. We passed through unmeasurable tracts of enlightened space, through many bright and glorious worlds, through many hosts of innumerable angels and spirits that seemed to be inexpressibly happy. . . .

"I looked and behind the garden of Eden. . . . There I beheld Adam and Eve walking in the garden. . . . Then another scene opened to me. I saw the Holy Jesus, an infant babe lying in his cradle, and his mother, in raptures of holy joy and humble love. . . . I saw him eat his last supper with his disciples, going out with them, and entering into the garden of Gethsemane. . . . I saw him bounded . . . and nailed to the cross. . . . I saw the body of Jesus taken down from the cross and laid in the sepulcher. . . . I saw him enter into glory, and sit down at his father's right hand."[13]

# Notes

1. Erastus Snow, *Journal of Discourses* vol. 19 (London: Latter-day Saints' Book Depot, 1878), 273.

2. Orson Pratt, *Journal of Discourses.*, vol. 15., 26 volumes, (London: Latter-day Saints' Book Depot, 1873 1854–86), 242–43.

3. Joseph F. Smith, "A Sermon on Purity," *Improvement Era*, May 1903, 503–4.

4. Heber C. Kimball, *Journal of Discourses.* vol. 4 (London: Latter-day Saints' Book Depot, 1857), 2.

5. Philip Haskins, *A Sketch of the Experience of Solomon Chamberlain to Which is Added a Remarkable Revelation or Trance of His Father-in-law Philip Haskins,* (Provo: L. Tom Perry Special Collections, Harold B. Lee Library, Brigham Young University, 1829), 137–40.

6. Orson Pratt, *Journal of Discourses.* vol. 3 (London: Latter-day Saints' Book Depot, 1856), 101.

7. Joseph Howard Maughan, *[Faith-promoting Incidents],* (Courtesy of the Church History Library, The Church of Jesus Christ of Latter-day Saints).

8. Brigham Young, *Journal of Discourses.* vol. 13 (London: Latter-day Saints' Book Depot, 1871), 77.

9. Brigham Young, *Journal of Discourses.* vol. 14 (London: Latter-day Saints' Book Depot, 1872), 231.

10. Archie Graham, as quoted by Marlene Bateman Sullivan, *Gaze into Heaven: Near-death Experiences in Early Church History*, (Springville: Cedar Fort Inc., 2013), 119.

11. Joseph Smith, *Teachings of the Prophet Joseph Smith*, comp. Joseph F. Smith. fifth printing, (Salt Lake City: The Deseret News Press, 1946), 207.

12. Kris Mackay, *Gift of Love*, (Salt Lake City: Bookcraft, 1990), 53-55.

13. Trevan G. Hatch, *Visions, Manifestations, and Miracles of the Restoration,* (Granite Publishing: Orem, 2008), 25–26.

# Chapter Five

# A Grand Reunion

**W**HEN WE LEAVE this life, we will have a grand reunion with our departed loved ones. Some people are blessed to see Jesus Christ and Heavenly Father. A number of people also see ancient and modern-day prophets and Church leaders.

Knowing that we will be reunited with those we love is a great comfort and lets us look forward more eagerly to the next life. President Joseph F. Smith said, "What is more desirable than that we should meet with our fathers and our mothers, with our brethren and our sisters, with our wives and our children, with our beloved associates and kindred in the spirit world, knowing each other, identifying each other . . . by the associations that familiarize each to the other in mortal life? What do you want better than that? What is there for any religion superior to that? I know of nothing."[1]

## Reunited with Family and Friends

Nearly everyone who visits the spirit world mentions seeing departed family members and friends. Brigham Young stated, "We have more friends behind the vail [*sic*] than on this side, and they will hail us more joyfully than you were ever welcomed by your parents and friends in this world; and you will rejoice more when you meet them than you ever rejoiced to see a friend in this life."[2]

Joyous reunions with departed loved ones will be one of the most thrilling experiences we have when entering the spirit world. The Prophet Joseph Smith looked forward to being reunited with his family and said, "I have a father, brothers, children, and friends who have gone to a world of spirits. They are only absent for a moment. They are in the spirit, and we shall soon meet again. . . . When we depart [from this life], we shall hail our mothers, fathers, friends, and all whom we love, who have fallen asleep in Jesus. . . . It will be an eternity of felicity."[3]

## *David Lynn Brooks*

David Lynn Brooks had the privilege of seeing his recently departed wife. She was aware of his grief and told David that whenever he needed her, he should pray and she would be with him. During her visit, David was allowed a brief glimpse into the spirit world. He writes:

"I went in the house, turned out the lights and lay down on the studio couch to relax for a few minutes. I had no sooner relaxed when I heard a voice, the voice of my wife, she was praying. Oh! How wonderful to hear that beautiful voice which I recognized the minute she spoke. At the close of the prayer I was so tense I hardly dared breathe for fear of disturbing this beautiful experience. Immediately I saw a dim light filling the room, it was not a brilliant light but a soft light, then it began to part in the center like a curtain. As it parted, I saw in the opening the most beautiful sight in all the world, my lovely wife. She stood about four or five feet away from me and made no attempt to come closer.

"She spoke to me and said, 'Lynn, I have seen your sorrow and grief but it won't be long until you will be with me, that we might again enjoy each others' companionship and love; I have wanted to come to you before this, but only tonight was I given permission by the priesthood to visit with you.' She told me that my grief had made her sad and that I should try to be happy and whenever I needed her, I should knock or pray and she would be with me, although I may never see her again until I come into the world of spirits. She then invited me to look into the spirit world, and asked what I could see.

"I told her I could see a group of people seated in a room or hall at a table or at desks with note pads and pencils.

"She then asked, 'Do you know who these people are?'

"I told her I didn't recognize any of them.

"She then asked me if I remembered the people we had done the temple work for in 1929 and 1930.

"She and I had worked the entire winter gathering genealogy of her people and then we did the temple work for them. She then told me she had been called by the priesthood to teach the gospel to those people and that she was very happy doing that work. She then told me not to mourn, that she was always close by. She bade me goodbye. The light gathered from the two sides and was then gone. As soon as the vision closed, I was on my feet, tears streaming down my cheeks in torrents. This time, they were tears of joy; no sorrow now."[4]

## Luana Anderson

All her young life, Luana suffered from palsy and, as a result, had never been able to go to church or attend school. When Luana's parents heard about a new specialist that might be able to help their little girl, they set an appointment. Before seeing the doctor, they asked Patriarch Charles R. Woodbury to give Luana a blessing. The blessing he gave appears to be the catalyst for the young girl's visit to the spirit world, where she saw both of her grandmothers and her sister. Charles R. Woodbury recorded Luana's experience.

Luana and her parents arrived at Patriarch Woodbury's home on the morning of December 10, 1947, at ten o'clock. Her father anointed her, and when Brother Woodbury sealed the anointing, Luana sat perfectly quiet, which was extremely unusual. Normally she was shaking uncontrollably. In fact, Luana sat so absolutely still that for a moment her father thought she had died.

Even when the blessing was done and Sister Anderson cuddled her daughter on her lap, Luana neither spoke nor moved. Finally, Luana began to move, but she did not speak. The Andersons went home, but that night, Brother and Sister Anderson returned and asked to talk to Elder Woodbury.

"We had to come back and tell you of our experience," Mr. Anderson explained. "I noticed when we got home, Luana didn't say very much. Looking at her, I thought she looked better. I asked her if she felt any better and she answered, 'Oh, yes! Heavenly Father came down and took me up to heaven. When we got there, two men came out of a building. He said, "I'm your Heavenly Father. This is Jesus and this is Joseph Smith."'"

The girl's parents told Elder Woodbury, "Heavenly Father introduced her as Luana. She said they talked to her for some time. Then they said, 'Live a good, clean life and you'll be a missionary all your life.' She said they were wearing white clothing and they had a light shine out from them, so bright it hurt her eyes. They were all quite large men, especially the Prophet Joseph Smith. She commented on how good looking the Prophet was.

"After talking with her for some time, they called Mary. She [Luana] asked who Mary was. He said she was Jesus' mother. She described Mary as being a small woman.

"'Mary,' they said, 'this is Luana.' Mary, with a group of angels, took Luana by the hand and showed her around. She saw a Temple, a beautiful building of gold. They then took her to a school that was yellow brick, as she described it. She saw one room with all girls in it and one with all boys. She went into a room with all girls in it. A young girl who had never married was teaching the class. A little girl was reading. . . .

"As Luana stepped up, the little girl turned so quickly and said, 'Who are you?'

" 'I am Joyce.' Joyce was the little girl who had died. Joyce was wearing a red and white skirt and a white blouse with long sleeves.

"As they went on, she came to her Grandmother Anderson and another lady, sewing for an angel, as she called it. Luana said they had a machine similar to an electric machine, but it didn't have to be guided. Grandma smiled and spoke to her. Someone that Grandma called 'Helen' was watering flowers there. Luana said, 'They are so much prettier there than here. They are all ruffled and doubled.' Heavenly Father showed her some daffodils he had raised Himself. . . .

"She said she saw a lot of missionaries, soldiers, and everyone was busy. She saw one boy angel in particular, but she didn't know who he was. She said while she was talking to Heavenly Father, Jesus and the Prophet, she saw some dark animal curled up asleep and she was frightened. They took her by the hand and said, 'Don't be frightened. We'll take care of you.' "

Luana told her parents that "the streets were all gold and the trees had gold and silver leaves on them. She saw a beautiful tree that had no leaves on it, but was covered with pink flowers. She said after seeing all these things, Mary came and took her by the hand and said, 'Come, Luana, let us go,' and brought her back."

That was the end of Luana's experience in the spirit world but not the end of her story.

"The next morning Luana asked her father what his father's mother looked like. He said, 'She's a short, heavy-set woman.'

"Luana asked, 'Did she have a pug nose?'

"He said, 'Yes.'

"She said, 'Well, I saw her, too.' "

Elder Woodbury said, "We all felt a rich outpouring of the Spirit that day. We feel that this vision and testimony was given to us as a comfort and assurance that our Heavenly Father is with her. Since this experience happened, this girl's spirit leaving her body and returning, she has been normal. She's been able to go to Sunday School, Primary, and day school and now she's in high school, and a wonderful girl since that experience.

"Her parents wanted to know what I thought of it. I told them, 'This is a day that girl will never forget. She knows that people live after they leave this earth because she saw her sister and both her grandmothers and the Prophet Joseph Smith and the Savior and Heavenly Father.'

"In talking to her recently, I asked if she remembered that day, and she said, 'Yes, that's a day I will never forget as long as I live.'

"This testimony is given to show that people live on after they leave this earth."[5]

## Seeing Heavenly Father and Jesus

During their visit to the spirit world, many people reported seeing Jesus Christ, and a few were privileged to see God the Father.

## *David John*

David John's parents were devout members of another religion, and it was one of their greatest desires that their son become a minister. When David was old enough, he was sent to school to receive the necessary religious education. While he was attending college in 1847, missionaries from The Church of Jesus Christ of Latter-day Saints began teaching in Wales. David listened to their message, gained a testimony, and asked his parents for permission to be baptized.

Shocked and angry, his parents refused to give permission. His father even placed David under bond to keep him away from the Mormons until he became of age. Outraged, David complained to Elder Orson Pratt, president of the European Mission, who counseled the young man to obey his father. Reluctantly, David obeyed, cutting off all contact with the Mormons. He also complied with his father's request that he remain at religious college and continue preparing for the ministry. In January of 1856, David visited the spirit world and was allowed to see Jesus Christ in His glory. David writes:

"I dreamt that I saw an angel of the Lord. . . . His eyes were of a dark brown color, but full of glory. His voice was clear but full of power and authority. . . .

"The angel asked, 'Why are you spending your time in vain here? How is it you will not join the Church of Christ and spend your time there?'

"I replied, 'I hope I am in the Church now, am I not?'

" 'You know better,' he said."

The angel then showed David a glimpse of heaven. David saw Christ in all His glory sitting on His throne and also saw people being gathered so they could be judged.

David said, "The Saints seemed lovely, and all smiled. . . . But the other line seemed miserable and full of discontent, sorrow and grief, turning their faces from Jesus . . . [as though they] could not abide His presence."

Disturbed by his dream, David prayed for help and guidance. During his prayer, the same angel who had come to him before appeared again and said, "Thou wert foreordained before the foundation of the world to come forth in this age to assist to build the kingdom of God upon the earth."

David felt conflicting emotions. Although he rejoiced over this spiritual manifestation, where the truthfulness of the gospel had been so plainly manifested, he realized he'd been given a grave responsibility. He wanted to be baptized, yet he was afraid of how his parents would react if he joined the Church.

In the coming days, David began studying a pamphlet written by Parley P. Pratt, *Voice of Warning*. After reading it, David informed his parents, friends, and teachers that he had decided to quit college, be baptized, and dedicate his life to The Church of Jesus Christ of Latter-day Saints.

In June of 1856, David was set apart to go on a mission in the Pembrokeshire Conference [mission]. The following December, David was appointed to preside over the Flintshire Conference [mission], and was called as a second counselor to the President of the Welsh Mission.[6]

## Mrs. Dunkard

Mrs. Dunkard and her family were living in Huntington, Indiana, when they were approached by two Mormon missionaries—Elder J. H. Truitt and his companion, Elder Lawson. Mrs. Dunkard was curious to know more about this new religion and admitted that her interest came from a spiritual manifestation she'd received. In it, she had seen the Savior holding a Bible. Elder J. H. Truitt wrote down her experience.

"We conversed with them [Dunkard family] on the Gospel and related the glorious visions that the Prophet Joseph Smith received from our Father in Heaven, and told of the visits of the angel who was sent to tell him of the glorious work which he had to do; and of that wonderful book which was about to be brought forth, the Book of Mormon. The lady [Sister Dunkard] became much interested in our talk and said she believed in visions, for she had had one herself. We were very anxious to hear her vision, so she told it to us.

"While lying down on her bed, not asleep, her spirit seemed to leave her body and rose above it in the air. She could look down and see her body lying still there on the bed. As she ascended up she met the Savior standing above her with a large Bible in His hand. He said unto her: 'Lay hold of eternal life.' This He repeated to her three times. She then made a hard struggle to grasp the Bible and lay hold of it, but she could not get any nearer, although she tried again and again. When she came back again and found herself on the bed she felt disappointed at not being able to lay hold of that which she so much desired.

"Elder Lawson felt to talk to her about her vision, for we knew the spirit of the Lord was with us, and that we had been sent with a message of salvation for her. We told her that the Lord had shown to her what eternal life was; even to be with Him in glory, and asked her to lay hold of it. But she could not, for she had not accepted all of the word of God, and had not become a member of the Church that He gave His Son power and authority to organize."

The missionaries went on to explain that Christ is the author of our salvation and that all people needed to take upon themselves the name of Christ, for there is no other name under heaven that will enable people to partake of eternal life. Elder Truitt told Sister Dunkard that there was much truth in the church to which she belonged, but the full gospel of Jesus Christ had been restored by Joseph Smith and was now on earth.

Elder Truitt concluded this story by bearing his testimony. "I bear my testimony to the truthfulness of the Gospel and know that it has been restored, and it is in the Church of Jesus Christ of Latterday [*sic*] Saints."[7]

## David B. Haight

When David B. Haight was shown a panorama of the Savior's life, he did not actually see Christ but received a powerful impression that Christ was nearby. Elder Haight said his experience gave him a more perfect knowledge of the Savior's mission. Elder Haight's manifestation occurred when he suffered a health crisis, which increased in intensity until he was on his knees praying for comfort and relief. The siren of the paramedics' vehicle was the last thing Elder Haight heard before the pain ceased and he lapsed into unconsciousness. Elder Haight related,

"I was now in a calm, peaceful setting; all was serene and quiet. I was conscious of two persons in the distance on a hillside. . . . Detailed features were not discernible. . .

"I heard no voices but was conscious of being in a holy presence and atmosphere. During the hours and days that followed, there was impressed again and again upon my mind the eternal mission and exalted position of the Son of Man. I witness to you that He is Jesus the Christ, the Son of God, Savior to all, Redeemer of all mankind, Bestower of infinite love, mercy, and forgiveness, the Light and Life of the world. . . .

"I was shown a panoramic view of His earthly ministry: His baptism, His teaching, His healing the sick and lame, the mock trial, His crucifixion, His resurrection and ascension. . . .

"During those days of unconsciousness I was given, by the gift and power of the Holy Ghost, a more perfect knowledge of His mission. . . . I cannot begin to convey to you the deep impact that these scenes have confirmed upon my soul. . . .

"Immortality comes to us all as a free gift by the grace of God alone, without works of righteousness. Eternal life, however, is the reward for obedience to the laws and ordinances of His gospel.

"I testify to all of you that our Heavenly Father does answer our righteous pleadings. The added knowledge which has come to me has made a great impact upon my life."[8]

## Seeing Church Leaders

Many people mention seeing Joseph Smith and Brigham Young, as well as other modern-day and ancient prophets and Church leaders. With Joseph Smith as the Prophet of the Restoration, it is understandable that he is one of the leaders most frequently seen. Brigham Young testified, "Joseph Smith holds the keys of this last dispensation, and is now engaged behind the vail [sic] in the great work of the last days. . . . He holds the keys of that kingdom for the last dispensation—the keys to rule in the spirit world; and he rules there triumphantly."[9]

## Heber J. Grant

Heber J. Grant was only twenty-five years old when he was called to be an Apostle. Satan worked hard to make Heber feel unworthy of such an important position. To combat the feeling that he was undeserving of his new position, Heber spent much time praying. He was eventually granted a vision, during which he saw many Church leaders. Heber felt this vision was given to reassure him that he *was* worthy of the position to which he had been called. After he became President of the Church, Heber related his experience during general conference. He prefaced his experience by remarking,

"There are two spirits striving with us always, one telling us to continue our labor for good, and one telling us that with the faults and failings of our nature, we are unworthy. I can truthfully say that from October, 1882 [when he was called as an Apostle] until February, 1883, that a spirit followed me day and night telling me that I was unworthy to be an Apostle of the Church, and that I ought to resign. When I would testify of my knowledge that Jesus is the Christ, the Son of the Living God, the Redeemer of mankind, it seemed as though a voice would say to me: 'You lie! You lie! You have never seen Him.'"

In 1883, Heber said he was traveling on horseback through the Navajo Indian Reservation with Brigham Young Jr. and six or eight other men when he noticed that the road ahead veered to the left and that another trail led away from it. He asked the guide, Lot Smith, where the other trail went and Lot told him it went down into a gulley and joined the other trail further on. Since Heber wanted some time to be alone, he told Lot he would take that trail and meet up with the others at the end of it.

Heber then said, "As I was riding along to meet them on the other side I seemed to see, and I seemed to hear, what to me is one of the most real things in all my life. I seemed to see a council of heaven. I seemed to hear the words that were spoken. I listened to the discussion with a great deal of interest. The First Presidency and the Council of the Twelve Apostles had not been able to agree on two men to fill the vacancies in the Quorum of the Twelve. There had been a vacancy of one for two years, and a vacancy of two for one year, and the Conferences had adjourned without the vacancies being filled.

"In this Council the Savior was present, my father was there, and the Prophet Joseph Smith was there. They discussed the question that a mistake had been made in not filling those two vacancies and that in all probability it would be another six months before the Quorum would be completed; and they discussed as to whom they wanted to occupy those positions, and decided that the way to remedy the mistake that had been made in not filling those vacancies was to send a revelation.

"It was given to me that the Prophet Joseph Smith and my father mentioned me and requested that I be called to that position. I sat there and wept for joy. It was given to me that I had done nothing to entitle me to that exalted position, except that I had lived a clean, sweet life. It was given to me that because of my father having practically sacrificed his life in what was known as the great Reformation, so to speak, of the people in early days, having been practically a martyr, that the Prophet Joseph and my father desired me to have that position, and it was because of their faithful labors that I was called, and not because of anything I had done of myself or any great thing that I had accomplished. It was also given to me that that was all these men, the Prophet and my father, could do for me; from that day it depended upon me and upon me alone as to whether I made a success of my life or a failure."[10]

## Silas S. Young

Silas S. Young was camping one night when he was awakened by a personage who took him to the spirit world. While there, Silas saw his Heavenly Father and Mother, as well as ancient and modern-day apostles.

"In the year 1903 on the 20th day of February I was camped in Kyune Canyon getting out mining timber. My cousin, Howard Young, was working with me. He had gone home to Huntington for a few days and I was alone. My tent was nearly covered over with snow and it was a very cold night. I read from the Book of Mormon until 9 o'clock then went to bed.

"I had been asleep probably two hours when I was awakened by a call 'Silas.'

"I said, 'Here I am. What do you want?'

"And he said, 'Come with me.'

"I had seen this man once before. He had on a loose robe of a dark color and wore no shoes. Had a dark beard streaked with gray; was of a stocky build and broad comely features. (I have always believed he was the angel Moroni.)

"He led the way and I followed. We went right up in a northeast direction to a planet to the east of the north star. When we arrived there I saw a great multitude of people gathered together out of doors in a conference. They were in a valley shaped like a great amphitheater that is, in such a shape that they could all see to the center where there was a platform raised three or four feet high, and on this platform was a seat or throne and on this sat an old man probably 65 years old who had on his head a crown of jewels and by his right side stood a man about 32 years old. Both these men had full beards and looked just alike only that the one on the throne was older.

"While I looked in amazement someone in the throng asked 'Which of all the prophets that had lived on the earth was the greatest.'

"The one on the throne said, 'Jesus may answer.'

"And the young man said Enoch was the greater because he not only taught the theory of the Gospel but that he lived and taught the practical part and perfected his people.

"At this time the man who had taken me there said, 'Come, now we must go.' He accompanied me for some time and then said, 'You may go on alone now as you know the way.'

"So I went on for some time and then saw the tent. When I reached it I saw my body lying there in the bed. (Up until this time I did not know that I had left the body behind but supposed that I was all together.)

"When I entered the body it was cold, so as soon as I could I started a fire. When it became warm and it was possible to stop shivering, I reached out my hand and got the Doctrine and Covenants. It opened automatically to the 85th section, and the 7th verse which reads. 'And it shall come to pass that I, the Lord God, will send one mighty and strong holding the scepter of power in his hand, clothed with light for a covering. . . .'

"While I was there at that gathering I noted the twelve apostles that Jesus had with him in Jerusalem stood in a line at his right hand and next behind them stood the twelve Nephite apostles. Then there stood Joseph and Hyrum Smith while Brigham stood next to Joseph and the rest of the twelve next to him. Some of these I remember were Heber C. Kimball, Wilford Woodruff and others. I noticed that Peter was a large man and that James wore a full beard and was quite dark while John was of a fair complexion and resembled Jesus very much but was clean shaven.

"Paul has a very prominent nose and his hair was raven black. I also saw Abraham dressed in a tunic with a band around his head. Enoch wore a suit of clothes that were home spun just as my mother used to make on her hand loom except that they were of a green color that of grass or green peas. Enoch resembles Brigham Young very much in stature, had a very pointed nose and a thin upper lip and a very firm mouth. A man that you would know by his countenance that when he had fully made his decision there would be no change.

"I also saw a group of ladies standing near the platform the one in the center who seemed to be about 65 years old was the most beautiful woman I have ever had the privilege to behold. She seemed to be in authority there and I am sure she is our spirit mother. There is a very marked resemblance between her and the elderly man who sat on the throne. There was Mary and Martha and Mary the mother of Jesus.

"Eliza R. Snow who it was my privilege to know here. . . . There were some others in this group that it was not given me to know. Some tall graceful fair ladies that belong to the Nephite Era that are very fair and comely. Some of those Nephite apostles were fine looking men, very tall and of very fine countenance. I shall know Enoch when I meet him some where in the future.

"I want to leave here for the benefit of my family and kindred that I do know for a surety that God lives and that Jesus is the Savior of the world, and that God will bring to a final conclusion all the affairs of this world in his own due time, and he will save in his kingdom all those who serve him and keep his commandments. At the time of this visit to the other world it seemed to be spring as the air was balmy and the grass green; the flowers were in bloom; clear rivulets of water was running in all the ravines; nature was smiling and all the people were happy and enjoying themselves in such a peaceful happy way that I longed to stay there.[signed] Silas S. Young, Price, Utah."[11]

## Notes

1.  Joseph F. Smith, as quoted by Robert L. Millet and Joseph Fielding McConkie, *The Life Beyond*, (Salt Lake City: Bookcraft, 1986), 26–27.
2.  Brigham Young, *Journal of Discourses*, vol. 6 (London: Latter-day Saints' Book Depot, 1859), 349.

3. Joseph Smith, *Teachings of the Prophet Joseph Smith*, comp. Joseph F. Smith. fifth printing, (Salt Lake City: The Deseret News Press, 1946), 359–60.

4. Duane Crowther, *Life Everlasting*, (Salt Lake City: Bookcraft, 1967), 59–60. Used with permission of Horizon Publishers & Distributors, Inc.

5. Charles R. Woodbury, *Faith Promoting Experiences of Patriarch Charles R. Woodbury*, (Courtesy of the Church History Library, The Church of Jesus Christ of Latter-day Saints), 20–22.

6. *Biography of David John*, Leonard J. Arrington Collection, (Logan: Utah State University).

7. J. H. Truitt, "A Vision," *Liahona, The Elders' Journal*, Vol. 5, part 1, June 22, 1907.

8. David B. Haight, "The Sacrament—and the Sacrifice," *Ensign*, November 1989, 59–61.

9. Brigham Young, *Journal of Discourses*. vol. 7 (London: Latter-day Saints' Book Depot, 1860), 289.

10. Heber J. Grant, "President Grant's Opening Conference Message," *The Improvement Era*, May 1941, 314–15.

11. Silas S. Young, *Faith-promoting Collection*, 1882-1974, box 2, folder 64. (Courtesy of the Church History Library, The Church of Jesus Christ of Latter-day Saints.)

*Chapter Six*

# Aspects of the Spirit World

S OME FEATURES OF the spirit world are similar to mortality, but others will be quite different. One of the different characteristics of the spirit world is light, which is frequently mentioned by those who visit there. The light in the spirit world has an unusual, all-encompassing quality and appears to originate from God the Father and Jesus Christ.

Another commonly reported aspect of the spirit world is remarkable feelings of peace and happiness. The third facet of the spirit world that will be mentioned in this chapter is music, which plays an important part in our lives here and will continue to do so in the next life.

## A Place of Light

Light is an important feature of the spirit world. Some people describe it as brilliant and dazzling, while others refer to the light as soft and pure. A few say the light is so powerfully illuminating there are no shadows to be seen. Some visitors mention a bright light that surrounds angelic personages or emanates from cities.

In the scriptures, light is often linked with glory and intelligence. "The glory of God is intelligence, or, in other words, light and truth" (D&C 93:36). Gospel doctrine teaches us that the light that fills the spirit world comes from God (see D&C 88:6–13). When speaking of the New Jerusalem, John the Revelator stated, "And the city had no need of the sun, neither of the moon, to shine in it: for the glory of God did lighten it, and the Lamb is the light thereof" (Revelation 21:23).

## Sanford Porter

When Sanford Porter visited the spirit world, he mentioned how clear the light was even though he saw no sun, moon, or stars. He believed the light in the spirit world emanated from God.

Sanford Porter did not believe in God and believed the earth had come into existence through a series of natural causes and effects. He felt that people who believed in a divine being were fanatics and that any spiritual manifestations they claimed to have received were products of an overly vivid imagination or due to "phantoms of the brain." Over time, Sanford became utterly disgusted with religion, believing that each church looked out for their own gain and that the Bible was nothing more than a "printed bundle of falsehoods."

For some reason, Sanford began thinking about death. He found it disturbing to think that once a person died he became extinct, without any further existence. Sanford's account states, "He began to be harrowed up in his mind with this awful thought." Although Sanford hid his feelings from his friends, he began to obsess over God, his place on earth, and the awful thought that there would be no life after death. As his inner turmoil continued, he began getting up at night to pace the floor and ponder such questions as "Is there a God?" and "What is my place in God's plan?"

Late one night, matters came to a head.

As his wife and children slept, Sanford woke with troubled thoughts and, as usual, started pacing the floor. Finally, desperate to have an answer, Sanford bowed down and in great anguish of spirit cried aloud, "O, is there a God? If there is—May I know the way that is right?"

A voice answered, "There is a God and thou shalt be shown three times this nite [sic] the way that is Right that thou need never doubt."

The voice had been a mild one, yet it pierced Sanford to his core and caused him to tremble. Still, he remained skeptical. Hadn't he told people many times that spiritual beings existed only in the imaginations of the ignorant? Sanford became convinced that someone had found out about his recent anxieties regarding God and the next life and had come to the house to trick him. Striding to the fire, Sanford picked up a red hot poker. He went to the door and angrily flung it open to expose his tormentor. He saw nothing except a light snow, which had fallen during the night. There were no footprints.

Undeterred, Sanford went outside and circled the house but found nothing. He concluded the trickster had somehow gotten into the house during the day, hidden away upstairs, and then spoken to him through a crack in the floor. Picking up a candle and a cudgel, Sanford began to search, vowing that he would beat the perpetrator senseless when he found him.

Meticulously, Sanford went over every inch of the house, but his search was in vain. Something within the recesses of his mind began to stir, for Sanford *knew* that he'd heard a voice.

Finally, he reached the undeniable conclusion that God had spoken to him. He thought about the voice and how it had caused his whole body to shake. Sanford admitted to himself that at the sound of the voice, his emotions had undergone a remarkable change. The anguish he'd felt over the last few weeks was gone, leaving him at peace. Tired out, Sanford lay down on his bed.

The account relates, "In a twinkling as it were, he was caught away with lightning Speede [sic] from things of Earth. Thus with a conductor by his side, he found him Self [sic] Standing in a World of light (whether in the Body or out of the Body he could not tell). But to use his own language, he said, 'I felt of my Self; [with] my hands and thought it was no dream—that it was really my Self.'

"They Stood at what he called a Railing encircling a Body of light extending up so high that he could not see the top thereoff [sic]. This light was all in motion as it were, life dwelling in the light, he could see as it were thousands of miles so clear was the light yet there was no sun, moon, or Stars to be seen: he saw People, as numerous almost as the sand of the sea, seated around this lite [sic]. . . . All these were Bowing to the light with humble Reverence, full of prais [sic] and thanksgiving to God and the Lamb, those that were nearest to the lite [sic] were the most happy, even beyond description. All this impressed upon their countinace [sic] (he said) which surpassed anything he ever beheld in beuty [beauty] and loveliness: But farther back from the Body of Light they were less happy; even as the light shone less upon them.

"Thus he looked back until he saw those that were out in Darkness. And, oh the awful anguish of soul that was pictured on every countinance [sic]. They were in the attitude of wringing their hands and knawing [gnawing] their Tongues for pain. He [Sanford] could not indure [sic] the scene and thus turning, he inquired of his conductor who they were. His answer was that they were those spoken of in the Scripture Who were liars, whoremongers, Adulterers, etc. He asked if their torment ever would have an end.

"The answer was it had a beginning and it may have an end.

"He [Sanford] asked what the Light was that he saw to which all those were Bowing to, who were so happy.

"He said it was God. The Angel (or his conductor) went on telling him many things, even all that he wished to know about God and that which was written of him in the Scriptures referring him to many passages, giving him chapter and verse. he told him that there was no true Church of God then on the earth, that they were all out of the way. he was forbidden to join any of them.

"He [Sanford] asked if there would [be] a true Church arise.

"The answer was, 'There will.'

"He asked if he would live to see it.

"He [the angel] said, 'You will.'

"After he was told all he desired to know, the Angel said, 'Come, we must go back.'

"He [Sanford] looked from whence they came and beheld a Dark abyss. He said, 'O, let me stay.'

"His answer was, 'You cannot stay.'

"Said my Father, 'Why can't I stay?'

"Says he, 'You are not good enough.' . . .

" 'Will I ever be any better?'

"Says he, 'You will. You will occupy this mansion,' pointing to the one by which they stood. He [the Angel] referred him to the Scripture where the Savior said, 'In my Father's house are many mansions, etc.' " Then the angel said, "When thou art converted, tell this to the World."

Sanford replied, "They will not believe me if I do.'

"The Angel said, 'What is that to thee? Do as you are bidden. There is [sic] some that will believe. Come, let us go.

"In an instant they were on the wing as it were and he awoke, feeling a most singular censation [sic] through his whole System like unto that of a Person's Arm or leg becoming asleep, as it is called, causing a prickly sensation in the part thus becoming dormant as to the action of the blood. Thus it appears that his Spirit must have left the Body; and that which we thought was his Natural Body (as he stood in the World of the spirits) was the Body of his spirit."

Once he was back in his body, Sanford tried to wake his wife so he could tell her what he had seen, but she was in an unusually profound sleep. After mediating upon his experience, Sanford was again taken to the spirit world and saw everything he had seen the first time.

Time passed and years later Mormon missionaries came to the area. They talked with Sanford, who told them about his amazing experience and said he would not join any church because he'd been told the true church was not upon the earth.

Yet the missionaries knew something Sanford didn't—that the true Church had recently been restored. It had been organized only a few months before, on April 6.

The elders explained that an angel had appeared to Joseph Smith, who was then entrusted with restoring the gospel as it had been taught by Jesus Christ. Elder Carrol and Elder White bore their testimonies that The Church of Jesus Christ of Latter-day Saints had truly been restored and contained all the gifts and blessings that had been enjoyed by the ancient Saints, such as visions and the ministering of angels They explained about the gold plates and how Joseph had been directed to find them at Hill Cumorah. Elder Carrol and Elder White then presented Sanford with a Book of Mormon and encouraged him to read it.

After Sanford finished reading it, he had many questions. After answering his questions, the missionaries asked if he wanted to join the Church. Stubbornly, Sanford reminded them that he'd been told the true gospel was not on earth and until God told him otherwise, it was his duty *not* to join any church.

Again, Elders Carrol and White pointed out that at the time of his vision, the true gospel had *not* been on earth, but since then, it had since been restored. They reminded Sanford that he'd been told that the true Church *would* arise, and the elders bore testimony again that The Church of Jesus Christ of Latter-day Saints *was* the church Sanford had been told would come forth.

Still, Sanford resisted, saying he had no evidence the Church was true other than their testimony. He said he would never join unless he knew for certain that the Mormons had the true, restored gospel.

The missionaries continued to hold meetings in the area for a time, and Sanford attended them all. Then it was time for them to move on. At their last meeting, Sanford told them he hadn't yet received any manifestation that the Church was true. They urged him to ponder and pray about the things they had told him.

Hoping for a last-minute miracle, Elder White said, "If you are convinced that we are right, will you come tomorrow morning and let us know?"

Sanford replied that he would and that, if necessary, he would follow them to the end of the world if he felt they were right.

That night was a long one for Sanford. He stayed up late mediating on everything the missionaries had said, especially their parting words, which seemed to imply that he might be given a manifestation. But nothing happened. When morning came, Sanford began to wonder if the Mormon elders were like all the others, deceiving and being deceived. Then, without any warning, Sanford was caught up in a vision.

To his amazement, he saw the same guide who had conducted him to heaven years ago. The angel informed Sanford that the Mormon missionaries were servants of the living God and that their testimony was true. He also informed Sanford that God had recently set up His Church and kingdom on the earth and that it was his duty to embrace it.

When the vision ended, Sanford hurried off to find the missionaries. They had left the village, but he caught up with them while they were walking down the road.

Elder White looked at him with a smile. "Well, Mr. Porter, are you ready to join us now?"

He was.

While walking back to his house, Sanford told them about his vision. The elders made arrangements to have a meeting at his house the following day. Word went around that Sanford had been converted, and many people came to watch at the water's edge as the missionaries knelt and prayed.

Elder White then led Sanford into the water and baptized him. Sanford's wife and two children were also baptized. That night, another meeting was held and Sanford, his wife, and two of their children were confirmed members of the Church. Convinced of the truth, Sanford began to teach others about the gospel and brought many to a knowledge of the gospel.[1]

## Samuel Turnbow

While traveling to the spirit world on a narrow, illuminated pathway, Samuel Turnbow was warned to stay on the narrow way. Alarmed at the frightening darkness on either side, Samuel prayed for more light so he could see more clearly. His prayer was granted, and upon his arrival in the spirit world, Samuel found himself surrounded by a bright and glorious light.

Samuel's experience began after he went to bed. An angel appeared and told him, "Arise and go with me." Samuel and the angel then began traveling along a narrow path of light, which was in the midst of an eerie darkness.

The angel warned, "Keep in the narrow way of the light for on either side is death."

Samuel was unsure if the angel's words were an analogy about the importance of obeying the commandments and thus "keeping in the narrow way" or if it had a more immediate and literal meaning. Alarmed, Samuel prayed for more light so he could see the path better. The light became brighter, making it easier to see where they were going. Then a dark mass appeared. Frightened, Samuel prayed for yet more illumination, and once again the light became brighter. An even darker cloud appeared. Within it was great thunder and lightning. Terrified now, Samuel prayed for deliverance.

He writes, "My prayers was [sic] heard and the fierce elements were dispersed . . . and I found myself surrounded with a much more glorious light which caused me to rejoice."

After his arrival, Samuel said, "I came into a house where I saw the Prophet Joseph Smith preaching.[2] . . . He [Joseph] consecrated a bottle of olive oil and set it apart for the healing of the sick and the opening of the eyes of the blind and to bring the ears of the deaf to hear the words of God taught unto them and the maimed to walk. He anointed a sick woman and blessed her and she was made whole . . . and I knew that this man was a righteous man and a holy Prophet of God."

After this, the angel took Samuel into another room where John Smith, a patriarch and an uncle of the prophet, gave him a blessing. Then Samuel watched as "the Saints went through the temple and received beautiful white robes."

Seven years after his vision, in 1840, Samuel learned about and was taught the restored gospel. Samuel and his wife were baptized and moved to Nauvoo to be with the Saints. When the Saints were forced to leave their beloved city, Samuel and his wife went to Mt. Pisgah. While there, Brother A. O. Smoot and his wife, who had been through the temple, showed Samuel their temple clothes.

Samuel said he had seen such clothing before but not on earth. He told Brother Smoot that those articles of clothing were like those he had seen in his vision.

The following year, Patriarch John Smith gave Samuel his patriarchal blessing, which turned out to be almost identical to the one Samuel had received in his vision.[3]

## William Dudley Pelley

Suddenly and without warning one night, William Dudley Pelley left mortality and was escorted to the spirit world by two kindly angels. While there, he noticed an unusual opal light that illuminated the building. William relates his experience:

"In the Sierra Madre Mountains, near Pasadena, California, I own a bungalow. When I want seclusion . . . I motor up to this hide-away. In the month of April, 1928, I was living in this bungalow while writing a novel. . . . One night toward the last of the month . . . between three and four in the morning . . . a ghastly inner shriek seemed to tear through my somnolent consciousness.

"In despairing horror I wailed to myself: 'I'm dying! I'm dying!'

"What told me, I don't know. Some uncanny instinct had been unleashed in slumber to awaken and apprise me. Certainly something was happening to me—something that had never happened . . . [in] all my days—a physical sensation which I can best describe as a combination of heart attack and apoplexy [stroke].

"Mind you, I say physical sensation. This was not a dream. I was fully awake, and yet I was not. I knew that something had happened either to my heart or head—or both—and that my conscious identity was at the play of forces over which it had no control. I was awake, mind you, and whereas I had been on a bed in the moonless dark of a California bungalow when the phenomenon started, the next moment I was plunging down a mystic depth of cool, blue space. . . .

"Over and over in a curiously tumbled brain the thought was preeminent: 'So this is death?'. . . Next I was whirling madly. . . . Someone reached out, caught me, stopped me.

"A calm, clear, friendly voice said, close to my ear: 'Take it easy, old man. Don't be alarmed. You're all right. We're here to help you.'

"Someone had hold of me, I said—two persons in fact—one with a hand under the back of my neck, supporting my weight, the other with an arm under my knees. I was physically flaccid from my tumble and unable to open my eyes as yet because of the sting of queer, opal light that diffused the place into which I had come.

"When I finally managed it, I became conscious that I had been borne to a beautiful marble-slab pallet and laid . . . upon it by two strong-bodied kindly-faced young men in white uniforms. . .

" 'Feeling better?' the taller of the two asked considerately.

" 'Yes,' I stammered. 'Where am I?'

"They exchanged good humored glances. They never answered my question. They did not need to answer. It was superfluous. I

knew what had happened. I had left my earthly body on a bungalow bed in the California mountains. I had gone through all the
sensations of dying. . . . Now that I had reawakened without the
slightest distress or harm, I was conscious of a beauty and loveliness of environment that surpasses chronicling on printed paper.

"A sort of marble-tiled-and-furnished portico the place was,
lighted by that soft, unseen, opal illumination, with a clear-as-
crystal Roman pool diagonally across from the bench on which
I remained for a time, striving to credit that all this was real. . . .
Somehow I knew those two men—knew them as intimately as I
knew the reflection of my own features in a mirror. . . . They continued to watch me, with a smile in their eyes, when I got down
from my marble bench and moved about the portico till I came to
the edge of the pool.

"'Bath in it,' came the instruction. 'You'll find you'll enjoy
it.' I went down the steps into delightful water. . . . People began
coming into the patio. . . . As they passed me, they cast curiously
amused glances at me. And everybody nodded and spoke to me.
They had a kindness, a courtesy, a friendliness, in their faces and
addresses that quite overwhelmed me. . . . Think of all the saintly,
attractive, magnetic folk you know, imagine them constituting the
whole social world—no misfits, no tense countenances, no sour
leers, no preoccupied brusqueness or physical handicap—and the
whole environment of life permeated with an ecstatic harmony
as universal as air, and you get an idea of my reflections in those
moments. I recall explaining to myself: 'How happy everybody
seems!—how jolly! Every individual here conveys something
that makes me want to know him personally.' Then, with a sense
of shock, it dawned upon me: 'I have known every one of these
people at some time or other personally, intimately! But they are
sublimated now—physically glorified—not as I knew them in life
at all.'

"I cannot make anyone understand how natural it all
seemed that I should be there. After that first presentment of

dying—which experience had ended in the most kindly ministration—all terror and strangeness left me and I had never felt more alive. . . . I was quite content to stroll timidly in the vicinity of the portico by which I had entered this harmonious place and be greeted with pleasant nods by persons whose individualities were uncannily familiar. They were conveniently garbed, these persons, both men and women. . . . The big, broad-shouldered, blue eyes fellow in white duck who had first received me . . . kept an eye on my whereabouts and deportment. . . . I pledge my reputation that I talked with these people, identified many of them, called the others by their wrong names and was corrected, saw and did things that night almost a year ago that it is verboten for me to narrate in a magazine article, but which I recall with a minuteness of detail as graphic to me as the keys of my typewriter are now. . . . I went somewhere, penetrated to a distinct place, and had an actual, concrete experience. I found myself an existing entity in a locality where persons I had always called 'dead' were not dead at all. They were very much alive.

"The termination of this journey—my exit so to speak—was as peculiar as my advent. I was wandering alone about the portico I have described, with most of my recognized friends gone out of it for the moment, when I was caught . . . up, I seemed to tumble, feet first, despite the ludicrousness of the description. A long, swift, swirling journey. . . .

"Next, I was sitting up in bed in my physical body again, as wide awake as I am at this moment, staring at the patch of window where the moon was going down . . . a great weariness in my torso as if I had passed through a tremendous physical ordeal and my heart must accelerate to make up the lost energy.

" 'That wasn't a dream!' I cried aloud. . . . There was no more slumber for me that night. I lay back finally with the whole experience fresh in my sense but an awful lamentation in my heart that I was forced to come back at all—back into a world of struggle and disappointment, turmoil and misinterpretation, to an existence of bill collectors, unfriendly bankers, capricious editors and caustic critics. . . . It was tragedy, the coming back.

"I went about my bungalow in the days that followed as if I were still in a sort of trance. . . . I was not the same man I had been. . . . I mean this physically, mentally, spiritually. . . . I was peaceful inside."

William reported that after his experience, he gave up cigarettes, coffee, tea, alcohol, and meats, commenting, "I endured not the slightest distress in giving these items up."

Furthermore, William said his feelings toward other people changed. Usually, he was impatient and angry with others when problems arose. In fact, William stated that he prided himself on being a "good hater." But after his visit to the spirit world, he no longer felt or exhibited even the slightest ill will toward other people who caused him difficulties.

William continues, "At any rate . . . I know that for a limited time one night last year out in California my spiritual entity left my body and went somewhere—a concrete place where I could talk, walk about, feel, and see; where answers were returned to questions addressed to physically dead people, which have checked up in the waking world and clarified for me the riddle of earthly existence.

"I know there is no Death because, in a manner of speaking, I went through the process of dying, came back into my body and took up the burden of earthly living again. I know that the experience has metamorphosed the cantankerous Vermont Yankee that was once Bill Pelley, and landed him onto a wholly different universe that seems filled with naught but love, harmony, health, good humor, and prosperity."[4]

## Pervasive Feelings of Peace and Happiness

In the Book of Mormon, when Lehi saw the fruit of the tree of life—which represented the love of God—he said, "And as I partook of the fruit thereof it filled my soul with exceedingly great joy" (1 Nephi 8:12). Nearly everyone who visited the spirit world said they experienced overwhelming feelings of happiness, peace, love, and joy. These feelings seem to arise because of their closer proximity to God and Jesus Christ.

Apostle Francis M. Lyman spoke about the joy that we will feel after we die. "It will be all right when our time comes, when we have finished our work and accomplished what the Lord requires of us. If we are prepared, we need not be afraid to go, for it will be one of the most pleasant sensations that ever comes to the soul of man, whenever he departs, if he can go with a clear conscience into the presence of the Lord . . . We will be full of joy and happiness, and we will enter into a place of rest, of peace, of joy, rest from every sorrow. What a blessed thing that will be!"[5]

## Ivan Harris

It's not unusual for people to have conflicting viewpoints with members of their family. Such was the case with Ivan Harris, who was disturbed by a nephew who had rejected the customs and values of society and the Church. However, Ivan's feelings underwent a dramatic change when he visited the spirit world and experienced overpowering feelings of love and happiness.

When Ivan Harris experienced a medical crisis and lapsed into a coma, he visited the spirit world. Upon his arrival, Ivan felt overwhelming sensations of happiness and joy. These feelings were marred, however, when Ivan thought of his nephew and recalled how offended he'd been by his behavior.

Ivan thought to himself, "I cannot bear to be in such a wonderfully joyous place and feel all the love and caring that is here and continue to think such uncharitable and angry thoughts about my nephew."

Ivan asked to be allowed to return to mortality, where he hoped to speak to his nephew and end their estrangement. His petition was heard and Ivan was granted permission to return for a short time.

When Ivan regained consciousness, the first thing he asked was to see his nephew. Unfortunately, his nephew was not able to come, but Ivan asked other family members to tell his nephew that he loved him and forgave him. Ivan lived for eight more days and then passed away.[6]

## Edward Southgate

While in the spirit world, Edward Southgate felt love, happiness, and joy radiating from the people he saw. His experience occurred while Edward was attending a fast and testimony meeting in Philadelphia, Pennsylvania. Because he was serving as a patriarch in his stake, Edward was sitting on the stand during the meeting. Although he usually didn't give much thought to the next life, Edward said that on that particular day he was filled with a desire to know more about the hereafter.

While the opening song and the sacrament hymn were sung, Edward said his thoughts were fixed on the hereafter. As the blessing on the bread was given, Edward pondered on the words of the prayer and wondered what it would be like to be in the presence of God the Eternal Father. After drinking the cup of water, Edward put his elbows on his knees. Looking down, he rested his chin on his cupped hands and closed his eyes. Edward writes,

"Suddenly, I seemed no longer in that chapel. I found myself standing in the midst of a vast assembly of people all dressed in white robes. I was greatly impressed—awed is perhaps a better word—by their appearance. Somehow, in a way I cannot describe, their faces seemed to flow, radiating love and happiness and something far deeper and more powerful than happiness—JOY! There were quiet smiles all around but no laughter. Looking back on this experience I remember that I was not conscious of there being very much variation in the sizes of these people: in other words, there were none who were noticeably much taller or much shorter than the average. They were all looking in the same direction and there seemed to be an air of pleasant, even excited, expectancy among them. Subdued, almost whispered, conversation was going on. So subdued were their voices I was unable to catch one word that was spoken.

"At first I thought I was in a large auditorium but as I slowly gained a degree of composure following a period of great surprise and strangeness, I saw that there were no walls and no ceiling and I realized that we were out in the open under the canopy of the sky. And yet, although there was an abundance of soft but brilliant light, there were no shadows as there would have been if we were in sunlight. I found myself wondering about this as I looked around for the source of all this light and I came to the conclusion that it emanated from these people themselves. In their great love for each and their great joy, they actually radiated light, soft, pleasingly soft, light, ever so faintly tinged with blue. Gradually, as my eyes became more accustomed to the scene and my feelings of amazement and awe gave way to intense curiosity, I became aware that although I was among these people I was, in some strange way, not one of them. They were dressed in white robes. I do not recall ever taking my eyes from them to examine my own clothing but I have a rather strong feeling that I was in ordinary street clothes.

"It was also my feeling, at the time, that I was there as an observer and not as a participant in the gathering or the proceedings. In fact, nobody seemed to notice me standing there; certainly no one smiled at me or spoke to me. I am sure there were people at the back of me and also on my left but my attention was focused on those to the right and in front of me. And as I looked further and further into the distance I saw that we were on a vast stretch of land shaped something like a huge, shallow saucer. From where I stood it sloped very gently downwards to the center and beyond that and on all sides it sloped gently to the horizon. As far as my eyes could see there were people, thousands—hundreds of thousands—of people, people in long white robes, people whose faces radiated love and joy and soft bright light.

"Suddenly the whispering stopped. Silence! Absolute stillness! I could sense the hushed excitement all around me. All eyes, including mine, were now riveted on the center of this vast, seemingly limitless amphitheater. And then I saw it! A little above the distant horizon what at first appeared to me to be a very brilliant star was approaching, growing larger and more brilliant every second. Then I saw that it was not a star but a man. He emitted light far more brilliant than I had ever seen and yet it was not dazzling to my eyes. On, on he came, lower and closer, just as if he were on a giant, invisible escalator. The whole vast scene was now flooded with a brilliance beyond description and I stood transfixed with awe. He reached the center and came gently to a stop a little distance above the heads of the people.

"Suddenly, there rang out from the throats of that vast assembly a musical shout 'HOSANNAH!'—and almost immediately I was back in my seat in the Broomall Chapel, conscious of what was happening there.

"That musical shout 'HOSANNAH!' meant a great deal to me because it brought forcibly to my mind memories of my membership in the Tabernacle Choir from about 1918 to 1925 or 1926. When first I joined the Choir that great musician and composer, Evan Stephens, was its conductor. He wrote and composed his beautiful 'Hosannah Anthem' especially for the dedication of the Great Temple in Salt Lake City and I think it has been sung at the dedication of every Temple built since then. It begins very thrillingly with 'Hosannah! Hosannah!! Hosannah!!! To God and The Lamb.' At one time Evan Stephens arranged for every Ward Choir in the Salt Lake Valley to learn the 'Hosannah Anthem' and the Tabernacle Choir also polished up its rendition of it. When all were ready these choirs assembled in the Tabernacle, the Tabernacle Choir members in their regular seats, the ward choirs occupying the entire balcony. I shall never forget that night. . . .

"So, as I sat in the Broomall Ward Chapel after the experience related above, my thoughts were of that massing of choirs in the

Tabernacle and of other groups and individuals with whom I sang in those happy days of the past when I could really sing, and I thought and thought of how wonderful it would be to sing in the Heavenly choirs of the future. (I pray that I may be worthy of that glorious privilege.) . . .

"This is a true statement. Signed A. Edward Southgate."[7]

## Music

A number of people reported hearing glorious music when visiting the spirit world. The music is said to be more beautiful than any heard on earth. Music is one way people can commune with God. The Lord said, "My soul delighteth in the song of the heart; yea, the song of the righteous is a prayer unto me" (D&C 25:12).

Because music has such great power to touch people's hearts, it stands to reason that it will be an important part of the next life. In the Book of Mormon, Alma the Younger states that after being released from the awful pains of hell, he saw "God sitting upon his throne, surrounded with numberless concourses of angels, in the attitude of singing and praising their God" (Alma 36:22).

## *Charles Woodbury*

When Patriarch Charles R. Woodbury stood to speak at a funeral for a friend, John Lovell, he had a sudden and unexpected glimpse into the spirit world. He proceeded to tell the audience about it, addressing part of his remarks to the choir director, Eddie Q. Dutson, who was leading the music for the funeral. Charles relates,

"When I stood up to start talking . . . it was revealed to me, and I said, 'Brother Dutson, you are fulfilling a promise you made in the Spirit World. When Brother Lovell left the Spirit World, you were chorister there. Many of these men and women in your choir today were there with you, and you promised there that when Brother Lovell's mission was finished on the earth, you would lead the choir again for him when he departed this life. Brother Dutson, you're fulfilling today the promise you made in the Spirit life, so Brother Lovell's rejoicing. He and his family all rejoice, and you shall rejoice, and the members of your choir, to think that you had the privilege of singing for that wonderful man's services when he left the Spirit World and came and completed a wonderful mission on the earth, and now that same privilege has come to you again, to sing songs to comfort his family. You're free now. You've filled the promise you made and I bear testimony to you people in this congregation that this is the case, that people come together, services are held, speakers speak to wish God's speed as they come to earth, and choirs sing songs.'

"This was revealed to me and I bear testimony that it is true. Not only in the case of Brother Lovell, but others. As they depart to come to this earth, to help them, notwithstanding that they have no recollection of any thing that transpired in the Spirit World, to come to this earth to be proven and tested and tried and to work out their salvation.

"I bear testimony to you that this is true, as it was revealed to me in the case of Brother Lovell. I have also seen Jonathan B. Pratt, who was the Bishop of the Hinckley Ward when we moved here. After he passed away, I saw him in vision. He was standing in a pulpit and the building was full of people. A voice said to me, 'This is Jonathan B. Pratt, presiding as a Bishop in the Spirit World, and these people in this building are members of his ward.' And I saw Brother Pratt as he was Bishop when he came, and I saw him as plain as I ever did in my life."[8]

## Notes

1. Nathan Tanner Porter, *Reminiscences [ca.1879]*, (Courtesy of the Church History Library, The Church of Jesus Christ of Latter-day Saints).
2. Samuel wrote about his vision *after* he had joined the Church and became acquainted with the Prophet Joseph Smith. At the time of his vision, Samuel saw a stranger and was told the man was a prophet of

God. It wasn't until years later, when Samuel met the Prophet Joseph Smith, that he recognized him as the man he'd seen in his vision.

3. *Genealogical and Blessing Book of Samuel Turnbow,* (Provo: L. Tom Perry Special Collections, Harold B. Lee Library, Brigham Young University), 37–38.

4. William Dudley Pelley, "Seven Minutes in Eternity," *Faith-promoting collection 1882-1974,* Box 2, Folder 104, (Courtesy of the Church History Library, The Church of Jesus Christ of Latter-day Saints).

5. Francis M. Lyman, Conference Report, October 1909, 19.

6. Norma Clark Larsen, *His Everlasting Love; Stories of the Father's Help to His Children* (Bountiful: Horizon Publishers, 1977), 104–5. Used with permission of Horizon Publishers & Distributors, Inc.

7. Alfred Edward Southgate, *Statement, 1976 Sep,* (Courtesy of the Church History Library, The Church of Jesus Christ of Latter-day Saints).

8. Charles R. Woodbury, *Faith Promoting Experiences of Patriarch Charles R. Woodbury,* (Courtesy of the Church History Library, The Church of Jesus Christ of Latter-day Saints).

*Chapter Seven*

# The Spirit World Is a Beautiful Place

ITHOUT EXCEPTION, THOSE who visit the spirit world are awed by its incredible beauty and splendor. Visitors report that although the spirit world is somewhat similar to mortality, it is by far more grand and glorious than anything on earth. Many people said it was so beautiful they didn't have the words to describe it. Brigham Young stated, "I have been near enough to understand eternity so that I have had to exercise a great deal more faith to desire to live than I ever exercised in my whole life to live. The brightness and glory of the next apartment is inexpressible."[1]

## Flowers, Trees, and Vegetation

Most visitors to the spirit world report seeing a wider variety of flowers and vegetation than exists in mortality and say the flowers, trees, rivers, and woodlands are more striking than what we have in mortality. A few visitors reported that many flowers there are unusual and of a type not seen on earth.

Many people who had near-death experiences also extolled the beauty of the spirit world. One of the more well-known experiences is that of Jedediah M. Grant, who served as a counselor to Brigham Young. After coming back from the spirit world, Jedediah said, "I have seen good gardens on this earth, but I never saw any to compare with those that were there. I saw flowers of numerous kinds and some with from fifty to a hundred different colored flowers growing upon one stalk."[2]

## John Powell

In 1867, John Powell and his wife, Fanny, were living in a schoolhouse in northern Utah when he was allowed to see the spirit world. John said it was so beautiful that he wanted to stay. He writes,

"I was lying on the bed in the Cedar Springs School House, when a personage came to me and said, 'Come!'

"My spirit then left my body and went with my guide. . . . Here I beheld the inhabitants. The houses and trees were beautiful to behold. I was so amazed and delighted that I requested my guide to permit me to stay and dwell there, for all things were far in advance of this world that I wanted to stay.

"He answered, 'No,' and said, 'Come!'

"He then took me to the next kingdom which so far exceeded the first in beauty and glory that I was again amazed and requested the permission to stay.

"I cannot command language to describe the beauty of the inhabitants and scenery, but my guide said, 'No, come!'

"He then took me to the next kingdom which was far more beautiful in glory and order than the former two. The beautiful flowers, trees, gardens, houses, people who were dressed in pure white, and so pure that I was overwhelmed with joy and most earnestly implored my guide to allow me to stay, but he said, 'You cannot go any further for this is next to the throne of God.'

"He then said, 'Come!' He then brought me again to this earth.

"When I saw my body lying on the bed I did not want to enter it again for I felt so happy out of it that I could not bear the thought of entering it again, but he said, 'Enter,' and I had to obey. Then I found myself the same as I was before he came to me."

After his experience, John Powell remarked, "By seeing the different degrees of glory I had no more desire to live. I would rather pass away for I was so filled with the scenes of bliss that I had no more desire for this world as it is. Having these thoughts on my mind continuously the Lord opened the vision of my mind, and lo and behold! a beautiful temple stood before me. I saw many people going to the Temple. I went into it and there I saw my wife, Fanny, dressed in her priestly robes. . . .

"I learned by this manifestation that I was not qualified but had to receive the blessings of the administrations of the Holy Temple in this life before I could enjoy those degrees of glory that I had seen. This knowledge caused a change in my feelings. I then desired to live that I might prove myself worthy before God and my brethren, and attend to those ordinances that He had ordained for the salvation of the dead as well as the living."[3]

## Mary Johnson Shumway

Mary Johnson Shumway talked about the lovely flowers and landscaping, saying everything was heavenly and glorious. She writes,

"About the 6th of April, 1891, in Pinedale, Apache Country, Arizona, I had been ailing quite a long while, and a deep gloom was over me. I had doctored for my troubles as best I could, but it seemed to do no good. . . . I had no appetite, and this trouble had been preying on me about two weeks, when one day I felt so bad I went to bed. A terrible feeling came over me. I felt it coming up from my feet and I was in a terrible sweat. I sweat so much the sheets had to be changed. It was different from any ordinary sickness, and it lasted through the day until nearly night.

"I sent for the elders to administer to me, but it did not seem to ease me and I grew weaker and worse with the sweating. In the evening it seemed that all of a sudden something fell on me and crushed me. The lady attending me, Lettie Bryan, saw something had happened to me and she called my husband. He came in and took me in his arms, and then it became all dark to me as far as this world was concerned.

"A light shone around me and about me, and the veil was raised so that I could see into the spirit world. I saw a great multitude of people, and I looked beyond them to what seemed like a sea of glass. As far as I could see there were beautiful flowers and shrubbery and artistic landscaping, and everything was so heavenly and glorious. –I couldn't tell about it; not even about what I saw, but I said, 'I am now in a bright light.'

"I then told my husband what I wanted to do with the children because I was going to go. At that moment the light left me and went right through the roof of the house, and I was aware of myself lying on the bed again. I told them to bring my children to me because I was going to leave. I had seen all these things, and I did not want to live here any longer, —that was the feeling I had.

"The children and my friends came in and surrounded my bed. The house was crowded and full of people. I kissed the children goodbye and told them how I wanted them to live. They began to beg me to stay and asked why I couldn't stay. I told them, 'I guess I will come back and stay awhile if it is the Lord's will.'

"I felt that I had come back into a dark, gloomy world, far less inviting that the one I had just left. The elders got the oil and anoited [sic] me and stood around my bed and prayed for me. After they got through praying, I knew I was going to live. . . .

"That same night I heard heavenly singing as plain as if it were just in the next room. I heard all the parts very clearly. The hymn they sang was "God Moves In a Mysterious Way." I heard that singing once again after that, and asked the people near me if they could not hear it, too. It seemed so plain I thought surely they ought to be able to hear it. However, they said they could not hear it at all. . . .

"The lady, who attended me during this wonderful experience, had previously almost apostatized from the Church, but the next Sunday in fast meeting she arose and said she could not be more sure of the truth if an angel had come and told her, because of the unmistakable influence in the room while I was going through this experience with death. . . .

"I know that I could not possibly be mistaken in the things I have told about in this experience. I have felt the influence of it all my life since that time and they are still as true to me as can be. It has given me great faith in the Lord to know that His children may know that He is, and that there is a wonderful dwelling place and a great reward awaiting us in the hereafter."[4]

## Animals

We know from Church doctrine that animals have spirits and possess intelligence. A number of people reported seeing a variety of animals and insects in the spirit world, including dogs, deer, fish, and even butterflies. Orson Pratt said, "The spirits of fish, birds, beasts, insects, and of man, are in the image and likeness of their natural bodies of flesh." He adds, "The whole [of] animal creation . . . are eternal and will exist forever, capable of joy and happiness."[5]

### Brother Pettersson

While in the spirit world, Brother Pettersson saw various animals. He saw not only lions, tigers, and lambs but also insects, such as bees and butterflies.

Brother Pettersson was a prominent citizen in a small city in Sweden. After he was "born again," he began holding religious meetings in his home. Because of his newfound zeal, he was upset in 1867 to discover that a friend, Mr. Carlsson, had been baptized a member of The Church of Jesus Christ of Latter-day Saints. Brother Pettersson promptly visited Mr. Carlsson to point out the error of his ways. However, he couldn't change his friend's mind and at the end of their discussion, Mr. Carlsson bore a fervent testimony of the truthfulness of the Book of Mormon and the divine calling of Joseph Smith as a prophet of God.

A short time later, Brother Pettersson had a spiritual manifestation that became the turning point of his life when he dreamed that he had died. Since Brother Pettersson knew the Lord spoke to people in dreams, he did not doubt that his manifestation came from God.

As Mr. Pettersson left mortality, he was met by kind messengers who "took him to the home of his ancestors, where he met his parents and grandparents, and other near relatives, and some friends who had assembled in his honor." Everyone was happy to see him and set out delicious fruit for him to eat. Although the language was different, it only took a few moments before Mr. Pettersson could understand and communicate his own thoughts.

After being taught many things, Brother Pettersson said "he was permitted to travel. . . . His guardian angel accompanied him, as his guide."

Brother Pettersson said the world of spirits resembled the world he knew on earth and said, "There were many countries, or 'kingdoms.' There were cities and villages, lakes and rivers, fields and gardens, houses and mansions, temples and palaces, flowers and animals of great beauty and variety. The people were busy. Some were building, some were planting, some harvesting. Many were preaching on street corners and in assembly halls, and all had large congregations."

When Mr. Pettersson asked about the people who were teaching the gospel, his guide replied, "They have been sent here to be ministering spirits to those who shall yet become heirs of salvation."

This confused Mr. Pettersson, who had assumed they were in heaven. The guide corrected him saying they were in the world of spirits. They approached a large congregation where the speaker had just concluded his remarks. A man in the audience stood, saying he disagreed with the speaker. Facing the crowd, this man told them they didn't need to repent and give up the things they liked to do. All they had to do was go to another kingdom. In this kingdom, the man said, no one had to take chances and no one would fail. He concluded by explaining that the leader of this kingdom was Lucifer. Some of the people were persuaded by his arguments and left with him.

The guide then explained to Mr. Pettersson that Lucifer had a large following and that the people in his kingdom were preparing to fight a final battle against the people who followed the Son of God.

They continued their journey and came to a park. Mr. Pettersson said, "There were all kinds of beautiful trees, bearing inviting fruit; also flowers that delighted the eye and filled the air with fragrance. There were animals of all kinds. Lions and tigers played gracefully, and lambs gamboled in an exuberance of joy. Bees hummed, and gorgeously arrayed butterflies flitted from flower to flower."

"This is Paradise," the guide told him.

"Paradise?" Pettersson repeated, confused.

" 'Yes, Paradise. You see,' the guide explained, 'this is the pattern of the Garden which God planted in the land of Eden. Adam knew this park well.' "

The two men entered the park, where many people were picking fruit and flowers. Some were simply sitting on benches. Everyone was dressed in white.

The guide explained, "These [people] belong to the Church of the Firstborn. They are of the King's household, and [include] invited guests."

As they walked along, the guide told Mr. Pettersson there was also a prison in the spirit world, although it was not a prison such as people had on earth. Rather, it was simply a different part of the spirit world where wicked people would stay until the day of judgment. The people who lived there were not allowed to associate with other spirits, because they might persuade them to be disobedient. He explained that while in prison, the people were meant to think on their lost opportunities. The guide remarked that although they were being taught the gospel, most of them had a hard time accepting it because of their current frame of mind.

Mr. Pettersson saw a man who looked familiar. The account states, "He strained his eyes . . . [saying] 'Is it possible? It cannot be. But it is! . . . it is.'" The man was Mr. Carlsson's older brother. The physical resemblance was striking.

In his written account, Mr. Pettersson explains, "This brother had died a few years ago in poverty. He was a 'Mormon' and had been ostracized on earth. And here he was draped in white, one of the King's guests, associating with the King's household!"

There was no time to talk to Mr. Carlsson's brother, as he was on his way to a banquet hall to attend a function being held in honor of Prince Emmanuel, but he told Mr. Pettersson that he might see him later, at a meeting that would be held at a place called Palm Grove.

Later, the guide escorted Mr. Pettersson to Palm Grove, where a large group of people were sitting under huge trees. A band and choir provided beautiful music. When a man rose to address the people, everyone went still.

Mr. Pettersson said, "It was evident that he was a commanding figure in the world of spirits. . . . He spoke of the Church in the desert, outlining the trials it had endured since the exodus from Nauvoo."

However, much of what the speaker said was incomprehensible to Mr. Pettersson, who had never heard of Nauvoo or how the Saints had been expelled from that city.

The speaker "went on to speak of the trials yet to come in the Valleys of the Mountains. But, he added, the Church will be triumphant, and the gospel of the Redeemer will fill the world. He spoke about the great Council presided over by the Ancient of Days, on which occasion power and dominion were conferred upon the Son of Man, and pointed out that the decrees of that Council were about to be executed.

"Then he spoke about the Millennium. 'That,' the speaker said, 'will be the reign of peace, when temples will dot the surface of the Earth, in which representative work will be performed, until every spirit in the spirit world shall have an opportunity to enter into some degree of glory.' "

Mr. Pettersson could not understand what was meant and said, "The speaker then went on to explain the different degrees of glory. There are, he said, in the world some who have received the testimony of Jesus, believed and been baptized and received the gift of the Holy Ghost; they have kept faith and been valiant to the last. They belong to the Church of the Firstborn; they are Priests and Kings, having received of God's glory; they are gods and the sons of God, and they are admitted to the presence of the eternal Father, and His Son, and the Holy Spirit. They shall come forth in the resurrection of the just with celestial bodies, and shall reign with Christ on earth over His people. They shall mingle with angels and the Church of Enoch and the Firstborn, and enjoy celestial glory.

"But, he continued, there are many who die in ignorance of the gospel, and others who hear it but reject it until they hear it again in the world of spirits. Among them are honorable men, who are blinded by prejudices. When they receive the gospel, they are in a position to receive terrestrial bodies and to enter into the presence of the Son, but not to receive the fullness of the father.

"Then, he said, there are a great many who do not receive the gospel on earth, nor the testimony of Jesus in the world of spirits, and yet do not deny the Holy Spirit. . . . Some are liars and . . .

sinners against the laws of chastity. They, consequently, gather in the kingdom of the devil and remain there until the second resurrection, when, if purified by suffering, they receive a telestial glory. They are in touch with the Holy Spirit, for they have not denied Him, 'but where God and Christ dwell they cannot come, worlds without end.' And yet, their glory surpasses all understanding. Each one shall receive, according to his works, 'his own dominion, in the mansions which are prepared,' and there 'they shall be servants of the Most High.' And their number is 'as the stars in the firmament of heaven, or all the sand on the seashore.' "

After the speaker finished, the choir and congregation sang a hymn. Afterward, Mr. Pettersson spoke with Mr. Carlsson's brother. Confused about the things he'd heard, he asked, "Who was the speaker?"

Mr. Carlsson's brother replied, "Joseph Smith, the great Prophet of the Last Dispensation."

When Mr. Pettersson woke, he was startled at first by his surroundings. But from that moment on, he was a changed man. Humbled, Mr. Pettersson realized he knew little about God's plan of salvation. But he was eager to learn more and knew just who to ask for more information—Mr. Carlsson.

"He hastened to the home of the rope-maker, the 'Mormon' whose testimony he had despised. . . . He heard again of faith, repentance, baptism, the laying on of hands, the gathering of the saints, the Millennial reign, judgment, and the glory of the Hereafter . . . he drank in every word eagerly. He and his wife and the older children were baptized."[6]

## Notes

1. Brigham Young, *Journal of Discourses.* vol. 14 (London: Latter-day Saints' Book Depot, 1872), 231.
2. Jedediah M. Grant, as quoted by Marlene Bateman Sullivan, *Gaze into Heaven: Near-death Experiences in Early Church History*, (Springville; Cedar Fort Inc.), 153–54.

3.  John Powell, *Autobiography and Journal, 1849 June-1901 Apr.,* (Courtesy of the Church History Library, The Church of Jesus Christ of Latter-day Saints).

4.  *Spirit-World Experiences,* (Courtesy of the Church History Library, The Church of Jesus Christ of Latter-day Saints).

5.  Orson Pratt, "Figure and Magnitude of Spirits," *The Seer,* vol. 1, no. 3 (1853), 33–34.

6.  J. M. S., "In the World of Spirits," *The Latter-day Saints' Millennial Star* vol. 79, no. 1 (1917): 1–7, 11–13.

*Chapter Eight*

# Structures in the Spirit World

*I*N THE SPIRIT world, we will not dwell on clouds but in houses. Those who visited the spirit world saw all kinds of homes—some were grand and glorious while others were more modest. They also saw schools and other buildings set aside for learning, as well as magnificent temples, amphitheaters built to accommodate large crowds, and other structures. Often they report that the workmanship and beauty of the buildings—inside and out—was exquisite.

Heber C. Kimball stated, "Many profess to believe that we have no spiritual existence. But do you not believe that my spirit was organized before it came to my body here? And do you not think there can be houses and gardens, fruit trees, and every other good thing there? The spirits of those things were made, as well as our spirits, and it follows that they can exist upon the same principle."[1]

## Homes and Buildings

Jesus said, "In my Father's house are many mansions: if it were not so, I would have told you. I go to prepare a place for you" (John

14:2). The following scripture from the Doctrine and Covenants infers that the type of home we inherit may be proportionate to our valiancy while on earth: "For they shall be judged according to their works, and every man shall receive according to his own works, his own dominion, in the mansions which are prepared" (D&C 76:111).

## Visiting the Spirit World

A man who held a position of leadership in the early days of the Church, whose name is not given, saw a number of homes in the spirit world. His guide pointed out the house occupied by Joseph Smith and another that belonged to his brother Hyrum Smith. The account states,

"A prominent brother in the Church had a dream a few years ago which was comforting to him even though its sequel was somewhat sad: He retired to rest one night in his usual good health, and soon fell asleep. He dreamed that his spirit left the body and proceeded, in company with a messenger whose presence was very pleasing, to a most beautiful country. The land was covered with the richest verdure, [luxuriant greenness] dotted here and there with houses of convenient size and rich proportion.

"He was informed by his companion that one of these residences was occupied by the Prophet Joseph, another by his brother Hyrum, and others by brethren whom he had personally known in life or whose names were familiar.

"He inquired if he might see these brethren, but was told by the messenger that they were not at home, their duties, which were very numerous and pressing, having called them to another part of the realm. The impression which this reply made upon the dreamer was that they were engaged in the important and seemingly almost limitless work of preaching the Gospel to the spirits in prison."

He asked if his daughter, who had died some time ago, was in this place and if he could see her. She was there in the area, the guide said, helping children who were playing a learning game. Although the man could see many groups of children, he couldn't see his daughter among the crowd, and the guide told him he would not be permitted to see her. Because of the joy he felt at being in such a beautiful place, the man was only momentarily disappointed.

He then saw two women approaching. To his surprise, he recognized one as a young lady who lived near his earthly home.

"He expressed surprise at seeing her, but learned that her present visit, like his, was merely temporary, though he learned that she would soon make this her permanent home.

"After a visit, the length of which was great when the sights he had beheld was considered, but so short that it lasted only part of one night, his spirit returned to its earthly tabernacle. He wakened his wife and told her that the young lady whom he had met in the other sphere was destined soon to die."

Several weeks later, he went to visit the young woman and found out that although she was very ill, she had no desire to get better. He gave her a blessing, and afterward, she whispered to him, "You remember having met me some weeks ago in the other sphere. Well, I am now going there to remain."

"Shortly thereafter, she quietly and peacefully passed away, and without doubt went to that delightful place . . . that was not lighted with sun or artificial means, but was made bright by the presence of the Father."[2]

## Cities

One way the spirit world is similar to earth is that both have cities. Within the cities are various neighborhoods, and it appears that people will be free to choose where they would like to live within the sphere they have been placed. The Apostle Orson Pratt spoke of this: "Beings that enter the spirit world find there classes and distinctions, and every variety of sentiment and feeling; there is just as much variety in the spirit world as in this."[3]

President Brigham Young corroborated this notion when he spoke of people living in the spirit world. "Yes brethren, they are there together, and if they associate together, and collect together in clans and in societies as they do here, it is their privilege."[4]

## *William G. Stone*

In August of 1891, William G. Stone was taken to the spirit world and saw a number of cities, including the City of God, the City of Enoch, and the City of Joseph, which was named after the Prophet Joseph Smith. William writes,

"While lying on my bed meditating upon the goodness of the Lord there appeared to me a heavenly messenger and he bade me follow him. On my compliance with that request my spirit left my tabernacle and followed him through what appeared to me a dark passage at the end of which seemed to be a very high wall.

"Being perplexed about which way to go, I was requested to turn to the left and ascend what appeared to be a very steep hill which I began to ascend with difficulty. When part of the way up, I stopped to rest. I thought I saw some one [*sic*] taking away my body and desiring to come back and take care of my body the messenger said it would be all right and that I must continue to follow him.

"I did so with great distress the hill seemed so very steep I felt I could not get up without help. Arriving at the top a scroll was raised and I was ushured [*sic*] into a Court with such Glory that I was overcome I became prostrated upon the floor the glory being so great I was entirely overcome. Being told to arise I was told I was in the valley of Redemption and I followed the messenger to what he told me was the City of Sacrifice for martyrs who had been slain for the Gospels sake.

"Turning around he told me to look and I beheld what I was informed was the Garden of Enoch in which grew all kinds of fruit that was beautiful to behold. The trees not being higher than the attendants could reach the top of them. The soil seemed to be full of the Glory of God not a weed to be seen. Through this garden ran a beautiful stream called Crystal river the waters of which was as clear as a crystal abounding in numerous fish of a silvery hue.

"In the garden were a number of attendants and a great many children all of whom were dressed in white tunics with scarlet and purple girdles around their loins the attendants wearing sandals instead of shoes and the children's legs were bare from there [sic] knees down having nothing on their feet. They were engaged in feeding the fish which were so docile they would come and eat from their hands and then they would bring a tribute up from the river and put into the hand of the children as a mark of respect for kindness.

"I wished to know how they watered the garden and why it was so clean from weeds and I was informed the curse had been removed that it grew nothing but that which was good for the use of inhabitants and was watered with dews of heavenly love. I saw among the fruit what appeared to be some very beautiful peaches that were so close I could almost reach them with my hands. The flowers were very numerous. I knew none of their names except the white Lily which was near me very numerous.

"I was led on by my Guide to where I could behold the city of Perfection or the city of Enoch which was situated nearly before the City of God. This city was presided over by Enoch and was of great magnitude and beauty. On the north side of which ran the sea Unity which also ran by the City of God. It's waters were as Placid and as smooth as a mirror the waters of which the lord caused to roll back to receive the City of Enoch not having been polluted by the sins of man. I was also informed the place where the city of Enoch came from. The lord had caused the waters to cover to prevent that land from ever being poluted [sic].

"This is what I was told. I also saw the City of God the Glory of which was so bright I could not discern the Holy beings therein but I was informed the trinity was enthroned therein.

"I was next shown the Celestial City on the right hand of the Son of God, the inhabitants of which were countless in numbers. . . .

"I was next led to where I beheld the city of Joseph all the inhabitants of which were dressed in white robes. I was shown the Prophet Joseph, Hyrum and Peter on whose brows were written righteousness, justice, and truth. There was [*sic*] seven steps that led to this city and each step was deeper as they ascended. It seemed with great difficulty for those who went up to ascend the higher step but I saw none fall back. Each step had a name, the first was innocence, the second simplicity, the third obedience, the fourth virtue, the fifth Charity, the sixth integrity, the seventh Purity.

"I was informed the Prophet Joseph presided over all the City of Joseph and had the guidance of all the saints on the earth and all revelation received here by the servants of God came through the Prophet Joseph. I was about to ascend the steps that led to the city but I was told I could not go there yet but if I remained faithful the time was not far distant when I should have the privilege of doing so. . . .

"I made inquiries for the two Bishops of [illegible] who had departed this life and was informed they were in the City of Joseph but I could not see them. They were laboring with the Prophet Joseph and their labors were very great for the salvation of those who had died without the gospel. No tongue or pen can describe their labors and everyone who receives the gospel by proxy added to their labors.

"I next inquired for my parents for whom I had done a work in the temple and informed they were in the city of adoption but was not permitted to see them and was informed they would be cared for under the direction of the prophet.

"There was a great throng of people going some to the city of Joseph and some to the city of adoption. Those going to the city of Joseph were clothed in white robes and were those who had been faithful in the flesh. The others who were going to the city of adoption had their work done by proxy after having received their gospel in the spirit world. I was then told that cities was as kingdoms [*sic*] to be presided over by whom the lord willeth.

"I was next led to behold the cities of misery which seemed to be as large as all the others put together which was divided into classes the innermost of which were murderers and those doomed to eternal perdition. . . . Their weepings and wailings were indescribable accusing each other of being the cause of their misery . . . those who had murdered any of the servants of god [*sic*] would have to remain in utter darkness untill [*sic*] the wrath of the servants of God would be appeased.

"This visit to the courts of Glory occupied about seven hours and a half. The Angel told me I could now return to my tabernacle and write what I had seen and heard and if I remained faithful he would call for me again and make known to me greater things than I now had seen, when I would want to remain. But I would have to return once more to earth."[5]

## *Lorena A. Wilson*

When Lorena Wilson was escorted to the spirit world by her mother, she saw vast cities, which were clean and beautiful. Lorena said she didn't have the words to describe the magnificent mansions, palaces, and edifices she saw, but she said there were buildings of various sizes and that they were designed differently than anything she had seen in mortality. Lorena states,

"At the time referred to [about three months after her mother's death], I had returned to bed between nine and ten o'clock at night. My husband was out to a High Council meeting which usually kept him to a late hour. A baby, six months old, was by my side, and twin girls two years older, lay in a crib in the same room. The latter acted restless and I was about to arise and look after them. There was rushing, as of wind, and a rustling as of autumn leaves that filled me with a kind of timid fear. Just then the room lighted with a soft white light and I wondered how the moon could be so bright as the room seemed lighter than at mid-day.

"At this point, I saw mother enter the door, looking as natural as life. She came directly to my bedside and greeted me. I had dreamed of mother visiting me and was disappointed when I [awoke and] found it was only a dream. Now I told her I was glad she had come while I was awake. She answered that she did come although it was a dream. As she was in spirit form, she could more easily converse with my spirit while my body was at rest. This time she had come, she said, to take me with her.

"I met with many surprises. There came with mother a large dog of the greyhound type. He came up to me and smelt of my hand then turned and smelt of mother's hand and showed an intelligent expression of pleasure. . . .

"Yielding to mother's wishes I arose to go with her. The dog took lead and leaped forward and upward through the air before us. Mother took my hand and we followed, mounting upward through space. . . . The arrival at our destination was like peeping over the summit of a large hill or ridge. Before us lay a vast city or realm, the full extent of which I did not see or learn. We seemed to be passing from east to west. It appeared like a beautiful morning after a rain. Everything was clean and beaming with radiant beauty.

"The ground seemed to be a kind of yellowish, sandy loam, and my thought was that it could not be blown about by the wind. We walked, or seemed to walk, but without apparent effort, a long distance through pleasant streets, lined with beautiful buildings, over paved walks which were bordered by well kept lawns. The lawns were set with pretty trees and shrubbery, with here and there beds of gorgeous flowers, which were a delight to behold.

"The first section we passed through was covered and closely set with large massive buildings as far as I could see. The domes and spires looked ancient, and I saw no gable roofs such as we have. The style of architecture was different from anything I had ever seen, impressing me as monumental in character.

"As we approached the section in which mother lived, there seemed to be a change in the style of the buildings. A newness and moderness was apparent. Very many houses were being erected, and I saw large quantities of stone in variety, that was in course of preparation for the builder's use. My language fails in any attempt at giving a description of the mansions, palaces and edifices I saw. They were of many grades and varying sizes, all different in design. I can only say that at every turn the scenes before us were glorious in their rapturous beauty.

"Then we reached mother's home, I saw it was constructed of beautiful white marble, or material resembling marble. The outside was completed, but the interior not yet finished. We ascended six steps at the front. The impression came that the steps were typical of mother's six children. On one of the steps was an ugly tobacco stain. Mother said she had tried and tried to erase it, but had not succeeded. (One, only, of her sons used tobacco.) The house, of modest size, appeared to me as being just what would please mother and be suited to her needs. I saw everywhere well kept lawns set with shrubs and flowers, in perfection of form and beauty of color. The flowers were of many kinds, clear and without blemish, and numbers of the varieties were new to me.

"The person I remember seeing first, on entering the city, was an old man engaged in cultivating flowers. During our travels I saw a good many old men engaged in the same kind of work.

"At one point in our travels I heard a wail as of one in deep distress—such a wail as pierces one through and through. Mother explained that it came from one of the spirits in prison. She showed me a portion of the realm that was covered with low, flat buildings in which spirits of the sinful were confined.

"At this juncture, I became curious to know something about the Savior and accordingly enquired of mother. She informed me that she had not seen the Christ nor been where He is. They were preparing for the great and terrible day of His coming, and were looking forward to that great event the same as we are upon earth. This surprised me as I had learned the dead go immediately to the bar of God to be judged, and supposed the righteous were permitted to see Him and dwell in His presence. The spirit world I learned is simply a step nearer Heaven than is this life—a little farther advanced.

"We next entered a large building with many rooms, a number of which I was allowed to visit. They were large, long rooms, and all were filled with children. I had not seen any children about the streets at all. But here the children were gathered as in a school and were graded according to age. The first room we entered was occupied by the infants and their many attendants. Some of the babies were hard to pacify, and all of them required close attention. In consequence a great many attendants were needed. One woman I observed with a tiny infant in her arms, which she was trying to soothe and comfort, but which continued to wail and could not be comforted. I wondered what caused the babe to fret and cry so pitifully.

"Mother answered: 'It is because of the close bond of sympathy between it and its mother. The mother is yearning after it and does not become reconciled in her feelings to her loss, or what she looks upon as her loss. If mothers could only understand what effect it has upon the child, they would not give way to such selfish grief and cause their innocent ones to suffer and their attendants to suffer with them.'

"In the second room I visited more little tots, and in the third room were children of the size of six and seven-year-olds. These seemed to be having a most enjoyable time. They were not only being carefully instructed and making rapid advancement in learning, but a portion of their time was being devoted to play. They were being taught how to play nice games that were new to me. One of the games consisted of rolling crystal balls through hoops. In this they were having a jolly time. . . . The full extent of the school, number of rooms, etc., was not shown me. One thing was manifest, the children were as happy as it is possible to imagine.

"One assurance also was given me, namely, that the children were contented and would not return again to this life if they could be granted the opportunity. While they did not grow in stature, they advanced in learning and intelligence.

"My account would not be complete were I to omit mentioning the sweet music I heard while visiting the children. It seemed to come from the rooms occupied by higher grades where they were doubtless being taught in the art of music. The sound was soft, soothing and delightful.

"During her last years mother had been president of the Primary Association in the ward where she lived, and was much devoted to her calling. Her labors were so much appreciated that the people felt like they could not spare her. The children were fond of her, and she of them. Here I found her also engaged in work among the children. She was a supervisor in this noble institution. She had been called from this sphere to fill that higher, holier mission, where her usefulness was greater beyond compare.

"Mother talked to me all the time I was with her, imparting to me many ideas that enlarged my understanding and gave me a different view of life. She taught me that I must not be afraid to die; that I should be ready and willing whenever my time should come. It is, she said, just as natural to die as it is to be born. In her own case she felt it was a privilege rather than a misfortune to die when she did. I must not think we have to learn everything here, nor remain till we reach perfection, for in the spirit world more rapid progress can be made.

"All should be reconciled to go at the proper time. I observed that mother could discern my thoughts, for as we went along she would satisfy my mind about things I desired to have explained without my asking.

"My visit must have occupied several hours, yet I was able to see and learn but a few things about the wonderful realm, or one of the realms of spirits, chiefly things in which my mother was interested, and in which I needed teaching. I found it takes time to learn even in that sphere of glory. I could not grasp and retain all that was shown me.

"One thing I should say before closing. The first thing I observed was the clear, healthy look of my mother, which was in sharp contrast to her appearance during her last days of sickness and suffering. Among the children, too, my attention was drawn to their vigorous, healthy and intelligent look. They were all well cared for. I did not see a neglected one. The same was true of the adults and aged. They all looked vigorous, and while there was a certain clean, clear, transparency noticeable, no where did I see any semblance of sickness or death. Such conditions, as a heritage of the flesh, had been left behind.

"I do not know how I got back to earth, but when I came to myself I was for a time in some distress. As I began to move, all parts of my body were in a condition best described by comparison to a limb which had been 'asleep' as we say. It was well on toward morning, and my baby seemed quite hungry, indicating that it had not nursed during the night. My husband had returned and was asleep. In such cases, where he came home late, he would retire quietly to avoid waking me.

"Since that happy experience my former fear or dread of death has left me entirely. I have not mourned and can not mourn for the dead, though I sympathize with the sorrowing. An abiding assurance had taken possession of me that the dead have only gone to a better place by far than this—a place of peace and happiness and of opportunity for advancement."[6]

## Temples

Some of the most glorious buildings in the spirit world are temples. Temples are sacred structures where blessings, covenants, and ordinances that are essential to a person's eternal salvation and exaltation are performed. In earthly temples, members of The Church of Jesus Christ of Latter-day Saints receive ordinances for their own salvation and do vicarious ordinance work for the dead.

Temples are just as important in the spirit world as they are on earth. Apostle Rudger Clawson said, "And so we have two great churches, one in heaven, the other upon the earth. They are moving along parallel lines, and the temple of God, it appears to me, is the connecting link that connects the heavens with the earth, because it is through the temple that we will be able to reach our dead, and not otherwise."[7]

## Heber Q. Hale

Heber Q. Hale wrote at great length about his remarkable visit to the spirit world. While there, Heber saw a beautiful temple topped with golden domes. He was told that the authorized representatives of families in the spirit world have access to our temple records and are fully advised of the work done here. He said the vicarious work done on earth does not become automatically effective in the spirit world until the recipients believe, repent, and accept the ordinances of their own free will and choice.

"It is with a very humble and grateful spirit that I attempt to relate on this occasion, by request, a personal experience which is very sacred to me. I must of necessity be brief. Furthermore, there were certain things made known to me that I do not feel at liberty to relate here. Let me say by way of preface that between the hours of 12 and 7:30 on the night of January 20, 1920, while alone in a room at the home of my friend W. F. Rawson in Cary, Idaho, this glorious manifestation was vouchsafed to me.

"I was not conscious of anything that transpired during the hours mentioned, except what I experienced in the manifestation. I did not turn over in bed, nor was I disturbed by any dream, an apparition, a vision, or a pilgrimage of my spirit into the world of spirit, I know not, I care not, I know that I actually saw and experienced the things related in the Heavenly Manifestation, and that they are as real to me as any experience in my life. For me, at least, this is sufficient.

"Of all the doctrines and practices of the Church the vicarious work for the dead had been the most difficult for me to comprehend and whole-heartedly accept. I consider this vision is the Lord's answer to the prayer of my soul on this and certain other questions.

"I passed but a short distance from my body through a film into the world of spirit. This was my first experience after falling to sleep. I seemed to realize that I had passed through the change called death and I so referred to it in my conversation with the immortal beings with whom I came into immediate [contact] with. I readily observed their displeasure at our use in referring to the transition from mortality, which word I do not now recall and I can only approach its meaning, as the impression was felt upon my mind, by calling it a New Birth.

"My first visual impression was the nearness of the world of spirits to the world of mortality. The vastness of this heavenly sphere was bewildering to the eyes of a spirit-novice. Many enjoyed unrestricted freedom as to both vision and action. The vegetation and landscape were beautiful, beyond description. Not all green, as here, but gold with . . . shades of pink, orange, and lavender as the rainbow. A sweet calmness pervaded everything. The people I met there, I did not think of as spirits, but as men and women, self-thinking and self-acting individuals, going about important business in a most orderly manner. There was perfect order there and everybody had something to do and seemed to be about their business.

"That the inhabitants of the spirit world are classified according to their lives of purity and their subservience to the Father's will was subsequently made apparent. Particularly was it observed that the wicked and unrepentant are confined to a certain district by themselves the confines which are as definitely determined and impassable as the line marking the division of the physical from the spirit world—a mere film, but impassable until the person himself has changed. The world of spirit is the temporary abode of all spirits pending the resurrection from the dead and the judgment. There was much activity within the different spheres and appointed ministers of salvation were seen coming from higher to the lower spheres in pursuit of their missionary appointments.

"I had a very pronounced desire to meet certain of my kinfolks and friends but I was at once impressed with the fact that I had entered a tremendously great and extensive world; even greater than our earth and more numerously inhabited. I could be in only one place at a time and accordingly it would require many, many years to search out and converse with all those I had known and all those whom I desired to meet, unless they were especially summoned to meet me.

"All worthy men and women were appointed to special and regular services under a well organized plan of action, directed principally towards preaching the gospel to the unconverted, teaching those who seek knowledge, and establishing family relationships and gathering genealogies for the use and benefit of mortal survivors of their respective families, that the work of baptism and the sealing ordinances may be vicariously performed for the departed in the temples of God upon the earth. The authorized representatives of families in the spirit world have access to our temple records and are fully advised of the works done there in, but the vicarious work done here does not become automatically effective there.

"The recipients must first believe, repent and accept baptism and confirmation, then certain consummating ordinances are performed effectualizing these saving principals in the lives of these regenerated beings. And so the great work is going on; they doing there a work which we cannot do here and we doing a work here which they cannot do there, both necessary—each the compliment of the other, thus bringing about the salvation of all of God's children who will be saved.

"I was surprised to find there no babies in arms. I met the infant son of Orson W. Rawlins, my first counselor. I immediately recognized him as the baby who died a few years ago, and yet he seemed to have the intelligence and, in certain respects, the appearance of an adult, and engaged in matters pertaining to his family and its genealogy. My mind was contented on the point that mothers will again receive into the arms their children who died in infancy and be fully satisfied; but the fact remains that entrance into the world of spirits is not an inhibition of the growth, but the greatest opportunity for development. Babies are adult spirits in infant bodies.

"I presently beheld a mighty multitude of men—the largest I had ever seen gathered in one place, whom I immediately recognized as soldiers, the millions who had been slaughtered and rushed so savagely into the world of spirits during the great world war.

"Among them moved calmly and majestically the great general in supreme command. As I drew nearer I received the kindly smile and generous welcome of that great loving man—General Richard W. Young. Then came the positive conviction to my soul that of all men, living or dead, there is not one who is so perfectly fitted for the great mission unto which he has been called. He commands immediately the attention and respect of all the soldiers. He is at once a great general and a great high Priest of God. No earthly field of labor to which he could have been assigned can compare with it in importance and extent. I passed from the scene to return later when I found General Young and his vast army of men completely organized with officers ever successive divisions and all were seated and he was preaching the gospel in great earnestness to them.

"As I passed on I soon met my beloved mother. She greeted me most affectionately and expressed surprise at seeing me there and reminded me that I had not completed my allotted mission on earth. She seemed to be going somewhere and seemed to be in a hurry and accordingly took her leave with saying she would see me again.

"I moved forward covering an appreciable distance and consuming considerable time viewing the wonderful sights of landscapes, parks, trees, and flowers, and meeting people, some of whom I knew, but many thousands of whom I did not know. I presently approached a small group of men standing in a path—lined with spacious stretches of flowers, grasses, and shrubbery—all of a golden hue—marking the approach to a beautiful building. This group was engaged in earnest conversation.

"One of their number parted from the rest and came walking down the path. I at once recognized my esteemed President Joseph F. Smith. He embraced me as a father would a son and after a few words of greeting quickly remarked, 'you have not come to stay' for which I understood more as a declaration than an interrogation. For the first time I became fully conscious of my uncompleted mission on the earth and as much as I would have liked to remain, I at once asked President Smith if I might return.

"'You have expressed a righteous desire.' He replied, 'I shall take the matter up with the authorities and let you know later.'

"We then returned and he led me toward the little group of men from whom we had just separated. I immediately recognized President Brigham Young and the Prophet Joseph Smith. I was surprised to find the former a shorter and heavier built man than I had expected. On the other hand, I found the latter taller than I had expected to find him. Both they and President Smith were possessed of a calm and holy majesty which was at once kind and kingly. President Smith introduced me to the others who greeted me warmly. We then returned our steps and President Smith took his leave, saying he would see me again.

"From a certain point of vantage I was permitted to view this earth and what was going on. There were limitations to my vision and I was astounded at this. I saw my wife and children at home. I saw Heber J. Grant at the head of the great church and kingdom of God and felt the divine power that radiated from God giving it light and truth, guiding its destiny. I beheld this nation founded as it is upon correct principles and designated to endure, and beset by evil and sinister forces that seek to lead men astray, and thwart the purposes of God.

"I saw vessels sailing upon the ocean and scanned the battle scarred fields of Belgium and France. In a word, I beheld the whole as if it were but a panorama passing before my eyes. Then there came to me the unmistakable impression that this earth and scenes and persons upon it are open to the vision of the spirits only when special permission is given or when they are assigned to a special service here. This is particularly true of the righteous who are busily engaged in the service of the Lord and who cannot be engaged in two fields of activity at the same time.

"The wicked and unrepentant spirits having still, like the rest, their free agency, and applying haunts and exult in the sin and wretchedness of degenerate humanity, to this extent they are still the tools of Satan.

"It is these idle, mischievous and deceptive spirits who appear as the miserable counterfeits at Spiritualistic séances, table dancing and Ouija board operations. The noble and great ones do not respond to the call of the mediums and to every group of meddlesome inquires. They would not do it in mortality; certainly they would not do it in their increased state of knowledge in the world of immortality. These wicked and unrepentant spirits, as allies of Satan and his host, operating through willing mediums in the flesh, these three forces constitute an unholy trinity upon the earth and are responsible for all the sin, wickedness, distress and misery among men and nations.

"I moved forward feasting my eyes upon the beauties of everything about me and glorying in the indiscernible peace and happiness that abounded in every body and through everything. . . . The farther I went the more glorious things appeared. While standing at a certain vantage point, I beheld a short distance away a wonderfully beautiful Temple, capped with golden domes, from which emerged a small group of men dressed in white robes who paused for a brief conversation. These were the first I had seen thus clad. The millions that I had previously seen were dressed, of course, but dressed variously. The soldiers, for instance were in uniform. In this little group of holy men, my eyes centered on one more splendorous and holy than all the rest. While I thus gazed, President Joseph F. Smith parted from the others and came to my side.

" 'Do you know him?' he inquired.

"I quickly answered 'yes, I know him' my eyes beheld my Lord and Savior.

" 'It is true' said President Smith. President Smith informed me that I had been given permission to return and complete my mission on the earth which the Lord had appointed me to fulfill and then, with his hand upon my shoulder, uttered these memorable and significant words;

" 'Brother Heber, you have a great work to do. Go forward with a prayerful heart and you shall be blessed in your ministry. From this time on never doubt that God lives, that Jesus Christ is His Son—the Savior of the world—that the holy [sic] Ghost is a God of Spirit and a messenger of the Father and the Son; that the destiny of man is eternal progress. Never again doubt that the mission of the Latter-Day Saints is to all mankind, both the living and the dead, and that the great work is to [be done in] holy temples for the salvation for the dead has only begun. Know this, that Joseph Smith was sent of God to usher in the gospel dispensation of the fullness of times, which is the last unto mortals upon the earth. His successors have all been called and approved of God. President Heber J. Grant is at this time the recognized and ordained head of the church of Jesus Christ upon the earth. Give him your confidence and support. Much you have seen and heard here you will not be permitted to repeat when you return. Thus saying, he bade me 'Good-by, [*sic*] and God bless you.'

"Quite a distance, through various scenes and passing innumerable people I traveled before I reached the sphere which I had first entered. On my way I was greeted by many friends and relatives, certain of whom sent words of greeting and counsel to their loved ones here. My mother being one of them. One other I will mention. I met Brother John Adamson, his wife, his son James and daughter Isabelle, all of whom were killed by the hand of a foul assassin in their home, at Carey, Idaho in the evening of October 29, 1915. They seemed to divine that I was on my way back to mortality and immediately said, Brother Adamson speaking:

" 'Tell the children that we are very happy and very busy and that they should not mourn our departure, not worry their minds over the manner in which we were taken. There is a purpose in it and we have a work to do here to which requires our collective efforts, and which we could not do individually.' I was at once made to know that the work referred to was a work of genealogy, on which they were working in England and Scotland.

"One of the grandest and most sacred things of heaven is the family relationship. The establishment of the complete chain without any broken links brings a fullness of joy. Links wholly bad be dropped out and either new links cut in or the two adjoining links welded together men and women everywhere throughout the world are being moved upon by their departed ancestors to gather genealogies. These are the links of the chain. The ordinance of baptism, endowments and sealings performed in the temples of God by the living for the dead are the welding of the links. Ordinances are performed in the spirit world effectualizing [*sic*] in the individual recipients the principles of the gospel vicariously performed here.

"As I was approaching the place where I had entered, my attention was attracted toward a number of small groups of women, preparing what appeared to be wearing apparel. Observing my inquiring countenance, one of the women remarked;

"'We are preparing to receive Brother Phillip Worthington very soon.' [Phillip Worthington died January 22, 1920. Heber was advised of his death by telegram and he went to Boise and spoke at Phillip's funeral on January 25.] As I gasped his name in repetition, I was admonished 'If you knew the joy and glorious mission that awaits him here you would not ask to have him longer detained upon earth.'

"Then came flooding my consciousness this awful truth, that the will of the Lord can be done on earth as it is in heaven only when we resign completely to his will and let His will be done in and through us. On account of the selfishness of men and the assertion to the personal will as against the will of God, many persons who might otherwise have been taken in innocence and peace have been permitted to live and have passed a life suffering and misery, or debauchery and crime, and have lived to their own peril.

"Men and woman and children are often called to missions of great importance on the other side and some respond gladly while others refuse to go and their loved ones will not give them up. Also others die because they have not the faith to be healed. Others yet, live on and pass out of the world of mortals without any special manifestation or action of the Divine Will. When a man is stricken ill the question of prime importance is not whether he is going to live or die, so long as the will of the Father is done. Surely we can trust him with God. Here in lies the special duty and privilege of administration by the Holy Priesthood, namely the Father concerning the one upon whose head their hands are laid. If for any reason they are unable to resign the Father's will then they should continue to pray in faith for the affect one conceding supremacy to the will of God, that his will may be done in earth as it is in heaven.

"To a righteous person, birth into the world of spirit is a glorious privilege and blessing. The greatest spirits in the family of the Father have usually been permitted to tarry longer in the flesh than to perform a certain mission, then they are called to the world of spirit, where the field is greater and the workers fewer. This earthly mission, then may therefore be long or short, as to the Father's will.

"I passed quietly out where I had entered the world of spirit and immediately my body was quickened and I arose to ponder over and record the many wonderful things I had seen and heard.

"Let me say here and now declare to the world, that irrespective of what others may think or say, I do know of my own positive knowledge and from my own personal experience that God is the Father of the spirits of all men and that he lives; that Jesus Christ is His Son and the Savior of the world and the spirit of man does not die but survives the change called death and goes to the world of the spirits, that the world of the spirits is near or upon this earth; that means individuality is not lost by death nor is his progress inhibited; that the principles of salvation are now being taught to the spirits and the great work of saving the Father's family among living and the dead is in progress, and that comparatively few will ultimately be lost and that the gospel of Jesus Christ has again been established upon the earth with all its keys, powers, authority and blessings, though the instrumentality of the Prophet Joseph Smith; that this is the power that will not only save and exalt everyone who yield obedience to its principals, but will ultimately save the world; that the burden of our mission is to save souls unto God. And that the work for the salvation of the dead is no less important than the work for the living."[8]

## Notes

1.  Heber C. Kimball, *Journal of Discourses*. vol. 4 (London: Latter-day Saints' Book Depot, 1857), 136.

2. "A Remarkable Dream," *Latter-day Saints' Millennial Star* vol. 58, no. 52 (1896): 823.

3. Orson Pratt, *Journal of Discourses.* vol. 2 (London: Latter-day Saints' Book Depot, 1855), 370.

4. Brigham Young, *Journal of Discourses.* vol. 2 (London: Latter-day Saints' Book Depot, 1855), 137.

5. William G. Stone, *Vision [ca.1891],* (Courtesy of the Church History Library, The Church of Jesus Christ of Latter-day Saints).

6. Lorena Wilson, *Life Sketch and Experiences of Lorena A. Wilson,* (Logan: Special Collections, Milton R. Merrill Library, Utah State University, 1932).

7. Rudger Clawson, Conference Report, April 1933, 77–78.

8. Heber Q. Hale, *A Heavenly Manifestation,* unpublished manuscript in the possession of Ruth W. Gregory, Phoenix, Arizona. Used with permission. (Copy also on file at Salt Lake City: LDS Church History Library.)

*Chapter Nine*

# People Are Active and Busy

EOPLE IN THE spirit world are happy and busily engaged in various activities and meaningful work. George Q. Cannon said, "Heaven is a place of activity, a place of progress."[1]

Many visitors reported seeing people reading, studying, attending or teaching classes, going to meetings, acting as missionaries, gardening, teaching children, and doing other activities that are common in mortality. Apostle Rudger Clawson said, "Sometimes people ask the question . . . 'What do the dead do?' . . . If I should make answer I would say that in my opinion they are doing over there just exactly what we are doing here. . . . The work that we are expected to do here, I am sure we will be expected to do over there, and we will have the means to do it."[2]

While in the spirit world, we will have opportunities to visit with others and enjoy friends and family. In the Doctrine and Covenants, we read, "That same sociality which exists among us here will exist among us there, only it will be coupled with eternal glory" (D&C 130:2).

Brigham Young talked about what people do in the spirit world: "They walk, converse, and have their meetings; and the spirits of good men like Joseph and the Elders, who have left this Church on earth for a season to operate in another sphere, are rallying all their powers and going from place to place preaching the Gospel, and Joseph is directing them."[3]

The most commonly mentioned activity is that of missionary work and teaching the gospel to those in paradise and in spirit prison. When Jesus Christ died and was resurrected, He sent missionaries "to proclaim liberty to the captives, and the opening of the prison to them that are bound" (Isaiah 61:1).

## *Wilford Woodruff*

At the Weber Stake Conference in October of 1896, Wilford Woodruff spoke about a time he was allowed to glimpse the spirit world. While there, he saw people rushing about energetically. The Prophet Joseph Smith was there, and when Wilford asked him why everyone was so busy, Joseph replied that time was short and they had to hurry to finish the work before Christ returned to earth. Wilford writes,

"Joseph Smith continued visiting myself and others up to a certain time, and then it stopped. The last time I saw him was in heaven. In the night vision I saw him at the door of the temple in heaven. He came and spoke to me. He said he could not stop to talk with me because he was in a hurry. The next man I met was Father Smith; he could not talk with me because he was in a hurry. I met half a dozen brethren who had held high positions on earth, and none of them could stop to talk with me because they were in a hurry. I was much astonished. By and by I saw the Prophet again, and I got the privilege to ask him a question.

" 'Now,' said I, 'I want to know why you are in a hurry. I have been in a hurry all through my life; but I expected my hurry would be over when I got into the kingdom of heaven, if I ever did.'

"Joseph said: 'I will tell you, Brother Woodruff. Every dispensation that has had the Priesthood on the earth and has gone into the celestial kingdom has had a certain amount of work to do to prepare to go to the earth with the Savior when He goes to reign on the earth. Each dispensation has had ample time to do this work. We have not. We are the last dispensation, and so much work has to be done and we need to be in a hurry in order to accomplish it.'"

Afterward, Wilford declared, "Of course, that was satisfactory to me, but it was new doctrine to me."[4]

## Isaac Brockbank

When Isaac Brockbank was allowed to see his wife, Isabella, in the spirit world, she told him she was perfectly happy and busy all the time. Isaac writes,

"I awoke about 4 a.m. Arose to see what time it was. I lay down again. No sooner had [I] done so [than] I found myself walking in a large park with beautiful trees [and] green grass. I had never seen anything so beautiful. I saw my wife Isabella. She was dressed plain of a light color." Isaac then asked Isabella a series of questions and wrote down her answers.

"Question: 'Do you know what I have been doing since you died?'

"[Yes.] She reproved me for not doing right.

"Question: 'Would you have liked to have lived longer if it had been the will of God?'

"Answer: 'If I could I would have liked to live longer.'

"Q. 'Would you come back if you had liberty.'

"A. 'I would not come back if I could.'

"Q. 'Did you think [much] about the children after you went away?'

"A. 'I thought [about them] for some time, but this feeling soon left me so that this thought does not trouble me.'

"Q. 'Are you busy?'

"A. 'I am employed all the time.'

"Q. 'Are you happy?'

"A. 'Yes. Perfectly happy.

"Q. 'Have you seen Joseph and Hyrum?'

"A. 'Yes, and many of the old prophets.'

"These were the questions that came to my mind. I was going to shake hands with her before we parted so I said I would like to shake hands with you, at which she put forth her hand to meet mine but when within about two inches of meeting a feeling went through my whole system as though I had received a shock only it was a glorious sensation."[5]

## Genealogy and Ordinance Work

One of the activities that will keep many people busy is genealogical work. Apostle Alvin R. Dyer spoke about the opportunities we will have for service in the next life: "Genealogical research will have a commanding position and will provide continuous opportunities of service and a labor of love that will instill happiness and peace to those who participate."[6]

The Prophet Joseph Smith talked many times about a "welding link" that exists between the dead and the living. He said, "The earth will be smitten with a curse unless there is a welding link of some kind or other between the fathers and the children" (D&C 128:18). He also said that our ancestors' salvation is necessary and essential to our own salvation and that "they without us cannot be made perfect—neither can we without our dead be made perfect" (D&C 128:15).

There is a clear link between genealogical work in the spirit world and in mortality. This important work goes forward on both sides of the veil, with much of it being done in temples. While we labor for the dead here in mortality, those in the spirit world do what they can to ensure the work goes forward by providing help and influencing us in ways we may not see or recognize.

President Joseph F. Smith saw the beginning of this great work. One day, he was in his room thinking about the Lord's visit to the spirit world. He said, "As I pondered over these things which are written, the eyes of my understanding were opened, and the Spirit of the Lord rested upon me, and I saw the hosts of the dead, both small and great" (D&C 138:11). As he watched missionary work commence, President Smith added, "I beheld that they [people in the spirit world] were filled with joy and gladness, and were rejoicing together because the day of their deliverance was at hand. They were assembled awaiting the advent of the Son of God into the spirit world, to declare their redemption from the bands of death. . . . While this vast multitude waited and conversed, rejoicing in the hour of their deliverance from the chains of death, thethe Son of God appeared, declaring liberty to the captives who had been faithful; and there he preached to them the everlasting gospel, the doctrine of the resurrection and the redemption of mankind from the fall, and from individual sins on conditions of repentance" (D&C 138:15–16, 18–19).

Later, President Joseph F. Smith said, "We are closely related to our kindred, to our ancestors, to our friends and associates and co-laborers who have preceded us into the spirit world. . . . those who have been faithful, who have gone beyond, are still engaged in the work for the salvation of the souls of men, in the opening of the prison doors to them that are bound and proclaiming liberty to the captives."[7]

There will be many in spirit prison who, after listening to missionaries, will repent and accept the gospel of Jesus Christ. However, before they can advance, they will need to have the necessary saving ordinances performed in their behalf. Because those in spirit prison lack a physical body, they cannot perform these ordinances themselves—the work must be done for them vicariously on earth. Mortals who are worthy can do this work in temples so those in the spirit world can receive the subsequent blessings.

Speaking of this important work, Apostle Rudger J. Clawson said, "The Savior stands for us. He has given His life's blood, that precious blood, that we might be saved. So we must stand for our ancestors. We must do for them the work that they cannot do for themselves. I call your attention to this fact, that that particular work is perhaps the most benevolent, the most charitable work in all the world, because they find themselves in a position where they cannot move. Their progress is stopped."[8]

## *William Butler*

William Butler had a spiritual manifestation shortly after the dedication of the Salt Lake City Tabernacle on April 11, 1852. At that time, he was told by an angel that the genealogical work was proceeding faster in the spirit world than in mortality.

William wrote, "Soon after this [dedication of the tabernacle] I had a vision. I was taken in the spirit to the spirit world where I saw many of the souls of men that had departed this life in all ages of the world. It was presented as the Saviour [sic] said, that in his Father's house were many mansions. I saw Joseph Smith and others preaching in the lowest hell and I also saw many that believed, but their penalties were not yet paid, and therefore would remain in prison and in chains whilst others that believed were allowed to come out into schools of greater intelligence where they might be taught principles thru the administrations of angels and spirits.

"The angel that was with me told me that the work was going forward faster in the spirit world than it was here, that they were waiting for us in the flesh to attend to the ordinances of the Gospel for them."[9]

## Learning Continues

The spirit world is a realm where we can further perfect ourselves, and once we arrive, we will keep studying and learning.

Even as our natural bodies return to the dust on earth, our spirits will continue to expand and grow in intelligence.

In the next life, we will be encouraged to study and gain knowledge. Brigham Young declared, "I shall not cease learning while I live, nor when I arrive in the spirit-world, but shall there learn with greater facility; and when I again receive my body, [after the resurrection] I shall learn a thousand times more in a thousand times less time; and then I do not mean to cease learning, but shall still continue my researches."[10]

Upon our entry into the spirit world, our ability to understand will be increased. Elder Orson Pratt taught, "We shall learn many more things there; we need not suppose our five senses connect us with all the things of heaven, and earth, and eternity, and space; we need not think that we are conversant with all the elements of nature, through the medium of the senses God has given us here. Suppose He should give us a sixth sense, a seventh, an eighth, a ninth, or a fiftieth. All these different senses would convey to us new ideas, as much so as the senses of tasting, smelling, or seeing communicate different ideas from that of hearing."[11]

Not only will our comprehension increase, but our memory will also be enhanced. Elder Pratt went on to say, "I believe we shall be freed, in the next world, in a great measure, from these narrow, contracted methods of thinking. Instead of thinking in one channel, and following up one certain course of reasoning to find a certain truth, knowledge will rush in from all quarters; it will come in like the light which flows from the sun, penetrating every part, informing the spirit, and given understanding concerning ten thousand things at the same time; and the mind will be capable of receiving and retaining all. I look forward to that enhanced capacity to learn . . . not only will I learn faster and completely, but I will actually remember it! We read or learn a thing by observation yesterday, and to-day or to-marrow [sic] it is gone. . . . Wait until these mortal bodies are laid in the tomb . . . then is the time we shall have the most vivid knowledge [and memory]."[12]

## *Mosiah Hancock*

Mosiah Hancock was born in 1834. After missionaries taught him the gospel, he was baptized. When Mosiah was a young adult, he had a vision where he saw people in the spirit world attending various classes.

"When about twenty-one years of age, I was permitted by the power of God, to go into His presence and into my former abode. I saw the Eternal Father on His throne. . . . I saw the Savior and knew Him. . . . Everything looked so natural and familiar. I seemed to have been a companion of the Savior and talked with him like a friend."

Mosiah was shown the premortal existence and saw Heavenly Father present the plan of salvation, Jesus offer to become our Savior, and Lucifer rebel. As Mosiah watched this panorama, he said that after Lucifer and his followers were cast out of heaven, spirits began leaving to go to earth.

Education appeared to be a high priority in the spirit world. Mosiah said, "During all this time the classes met frequently, being taught by instructors appointed. Each member knew his or her own place, and took it each time, and the best of order prevailed. They were taught in the arts and sciences, and everything necessary to make the heart happy. The teachers of the classes received the instruction they imparted from certain notable ones, who in turn got their directions from the Father and the Son. . . . I also saw Joseph, Brigham, and many others engaged in this work of education. I thought as some became more efficient that they were advanced from class to class."

When it was Mosiah's turn to go to earth, he asked the Savior if he could have the same position—that of a teacher—when he returned.

The Savior told him, "Yes, and greater, but you have to go down to the earth, and take a lowly position and be misunderstood by man, even your brethren and endure many hardships and set many examples of humility and patience, that you may return and enter the glory, even such as I have."

Jesus added, " 'Your time is now come to take your mission to the earth,' and He laid His hands on my head, as He had done to others, and set me apart for that important mission. He again said to me, 'I will see you safely thru [sic] until you return again.' "

Mosiah ended his account by saying, "I fully believe on that promise."[13]

## Teaching Children and Adults

Brigham Young said, "If we are striving with all the powers and faculties God has given us to improve upon our talents, to prepare ourselves to dwell in eternal life, and the grave receives our bodies while we are thus engaged, with what disposition will our spirits enter their next state? They will be still striving to do the things of God, only in a much greater degree—learning, increasing, growing in grace and in the knowledge of the truth."[14]

A number of experiences mention adults and children being taught in school-like settings. Church doctrine teaches that all children who die before the age of accountability (eight years old) will receive a celestial glory. Joseph Smith said, "I also beheld that all children who die before they arrive at the years of accountability are saved in the celestial kingdom of heaven" (D&C 137:10).

### David John

After David John saw the spirit world in a vision, he became converted to the gospel, served a mission, and immigrated to the United States. While living in Provo, Utah, he again visited the spirit world and was told he would teach young children. David wrote,

"I once dreamed that I departed this life and entered the spirit world where I witnessed the presence of thousands of spirits. I asked my guide how long would my body lay in the dust.

"He answered: 'Very much depends upon your faithfulness and energy. You have a mission to perform to preach and to administer to the spirit world. As soon as your work will be accomplished your body and spirit will be reunited.'

"In passing through the veil I experienced no pain or fear. The objects and sights around me took away all trouble and added to my former knowledge. I experienced more joy than ever before.

"My guide led me to an apartment where I saw thousands of children between the ages of four and eight years. He informed me that the first part of my mission should be to teach them to read and write. He handed me a book which was the classbook. I opened it and examined it. I could not read it and informed him so. He taught me to read the first one half of the first page which made me understand the whole book and I became a competent teacher.

"When we entered this department all stood up and made a salute after which they were seated. I was informed that I was to tarry with the multitude without an assistant.

"He said, 'I will show you how.'

"He taught me an exercise on the blackboard by which I could teach sixty thousand as readily as sixty which I readily adopted.

"He led me to the second department which appeared to be as numerous as the first which were from eight to sixteen years of age. He informed me that my mission to them should be to preach unto them the gospel and teach them the principles of life and salvation. When we entered this apartment they raised to their feet and gave a salute and he (the angel) said: 'You can call others to assist you after awhile.'

"We then entered the third apartment and found them more numerous than in the first two. They consisted of persons from 16 to 40 years of age. When we approached them they also gave us a salutation as the others did. I was informed that my mission to them was to teach them the gospel and to superintend over them and to have the priesthood conferred upon them.

"I was led to the fourth apartment. They were as numerous as the third and were men from 40 to 100 years old. I was commanded to preach the gospel to them and see that they had the priesthood conferred upon them and that their endowment should be secured and that I should call all necessary help to accomplish this work. They also made a salute like those before them.

"I told my guide that if I must accomplish all this work given me before my body would be resurrected, I feared it would be a long time.

"He answered me: 'Much will depend upon your diligence and perseverance. If the work would be attended to early and late it would be accomplished sooner;' but he added, 'it must be done, for they belong to you and when the mission is finished your body and spirit will be united and your joy will be full.'

"I awoke and found myself in Provo, Utah in the fall of 1867. Now in regard to this dream I wish to say that it was on the night of Nov. 5, 1867."[15]

## Notes

1.  George Q. Cannon, Conference Report, April 1899, 20.
2.  Rudger J. Clawson, Conference Report, April 1933, 75–76.
3.  Brigham Young, *Journal of Discourses*. vol. 3 (London: Latter-day Saints' Book Depot, 1856), 372.
4.  Wilford Woodruff, *The Deseret Weekly* vol. 53, no. 21 (1896), 642–43.
5.  Joseph Heinerman, *Spirit World Manifestations*, (Salt Lake City: Magazine Printing and Publishing, 1978), 141–42.
6.  Alvin R. Dyer, *The awakening in the spirit world*, (Courtesy of the Church History Library, The Church of Jesus Christ of Latter-day Saints).
7.  Joseph F. Smith, *Gospel Doctrine; Selections From the Sermons and Writings of Joseph F. Smith*, 13th Edition, (Salt Lake City: Deseret Book, 1963), 431.
8.  Rudger Clawson, Conference Report, April 1933, 77.
9.  William Butler, *"Journal of William Butler" in Autobiographies of William Butler*, (Provo: L. Tom Perry Special Collections, Harold B. Lee Library, Brigham Young University), 7.

10. Brigham Young, *Journal of Discourses*. vol. 8. London: Latter-day Saints' Book Dept, 1861, 10.

11. Orson Pratt, *Journal of Discourses*. vol. 2 (London: Latter-day Saints' Book Depot, 1855), 247.

12. Orson Pratt, *Journal of Discourses*. vol. 2 (London: Latter-day Saints' Book Depot, 1855), 246.

13. Mosiah Lyman Hancock, *The Life of Mosiah Lyman Hancock*, (Courtesy of the Church History Library, The Church of Jesus Christ of Latter-day Saints).

14. Brigham Young, *Journal of Discourses*. vol. 7 (London: Latter-day Saints' Book Depot, 1860), 333.

15. Joseph Heinerman, *Eternal Testimonies, Inspired Testimonies of Latter-day Saints*, (Manti: Mountain Valley Publishers, 1974), 167–68.

*Chapter Ten*

# The Gospel Is Taught

**M**ANY VISITORS TO the spirit world saw missionaries teaching the gospel. Because countless people throughout the ages have died without hearing the gospel of Jesus Christ, a great missionary plan has been established so all departed souls will have the opportunity to hear the gospel message. "For this cause was the gospel preached also to them that are dead, that they might be judged according to men in the flesh, but live according to God in the spirit" (1 Peter 4:6).

"Now, there are many of our ancestors who had no opportunity at all in life of hearing the Gospel," said Apostle Rudger J. Clawson during general conference. "That opportunity must come to them. How can it come to them? Only in one way, and that is by the preaching of the Gospel, and the Gospel will be preached to them . . . The work to be done there is vastly greater than that which is done upon the earth by the Saints of God. There are millions and millions upon millions who have lived and died since the Savior was upon the earth, down to the present time. The work must be done for them."[1]

The spirit world is a place of activity, and the righteous will be busily engaged in furthering God's work by teaching people and bringing them to a knowledge of the gospel. When speaking of departed members of the Church, Brigham Young said, "What are they doing there [in the spirit world]? They are preaching, preaching all the time, and preparing the way for us to hasten our work in building temples here and elsewhere."[2]

Apostle Alvin R. Dyer said, "For the true and devoted latter-day Saint [*sic*] there is much to be done in the Spirit World in a vast program to further God's work. . . . Righteous spirits gather together there to teach and testify unto those who will listen and to prepare and qualify themselves for a future day."[3]

The mercy of God is manifested in behalf of those who have not had the chance to hear the gospel. In his vision of the redemption of the dead, President Joseph F. Smith saw that righteous spirits were sent forth to preach the gospel to captives who were being held in spirit prison. "Thus was the gospel preached to those who had died in their sins, without a knowledge of the truth, or in transgression, having rejected the prophets. These were taught faith in God, repentance from sin, vicarious baptism for the remission of sins, the gift of the Holy Ghost by the laying on of hands, and all other principles of the gospel that were necessary for them to know in order to qualify themselves that they might be judged according to men in the flesh, but live according to God in the spirit" (D&C 138:32–34).

At times, people may be called to the spirit world to assist in important work, such as genealogy and teaching the gospel. In Heber Q. Hales's account (see chapter eight), he states, "Men and woman and children are often called to missions of great importance on the other side."[4]

Many accounts of near-death experiences also state that because of the tremendous urgency of missionary work, righteous people are sometimes called to the other side to assist in this work.[5]

Later in this chapter, James LeSueur indicates that his brother Frank was called to the spirit world to teach the gospel.

Elder Neal A. Maxwell explains that there is a great need for righteous people to teach the gospel: "On the other side of the veil, there are perhaps seventy billion people. They need the same gospel, and releases occur here to aid the Lord's work there. Each release of a righteous individual from this life is also a call to new labors. . . . Therefore, though we miss the departed righteous so much here, hundreds may feel their touch there. . . . A mortal life may need to be 'shortened' by twenty years as we might view—but if so, it may be done in order for special services to be rendered by that individual in the spirit world, services that will benefit thousands of new neighbors."[6]

Apostle Melvin J. Ballard relates an incident where a young elder was killed while traveling to his mission but stated that the young man continued his mission in the spirit world: "Some time ago a fine young elder, Elder Burt, received a call to go on a mission—he wanted to go to the South American Mission so he talked to me about it, and after conference it was decided to let him go to South America. On the way there he lost his life in the sinking of the *Vesperous*. I was distressed over his father and mother and I tried to comfort them, for the assurance came to me was that their son was still a missionary and that God needed him and was using him in a more effective way than if he had gone on his earthly mission."[7]

It appears that missionary work on the other side of the veil will proceed more rapidly than is currently seen by modern-day missionaries. President Lorenzo Snow said, "I believe, strongly too, that when the Gospel is preached to the spirits in prison, the success attending that preaching will be far greater than that attending the preaching of our Elders in this life. I believe there will be very few indeed of those spirits who will not gladly receive the Gospel when it is carried to them. The circumstances there will be a thousand times more favorable."[8]

Although the gospel will be taught in the spirit world, individuals will be free—as they are on earth—to accept or reject the message. Some Latter-day Saints believe that once spirits reach the other side and realize that life continues, even the stoutest of atheists will accept that Jesus is the Christ and that the gospel is true, but this is not the case. Agency has been and always will be an integral part of God's plan, and no one in the spirit world will be forced to listen to or accept the gospel. People will continue to have freedom to make their own decisions.

## Emelius Berg

When Emelius Berg visited the spirit world in February of 1886, he felt that he'd been called there to teach the gospel.

Emelius stated, "I found myself in the spirit world, and I saw a great multitude of people, in fact, millions upon millions of them. I thought I had come there to preach the gospel. There appeared to be several persons preaching the gospel, and hearing and seeing those persons thus engaged brought to my mind the object of my visit there.

"I then started in to preach the gospel of Jesus Christ as it was given to me. I taught them that those present should believe in Jesus Christ, as the Son of God, who had been there and introduced Himself as the Son of God, and who had been slain in the flesh. I promised them that inasmuch as they would receive His doctrine, work should be done for them upon the earth in the temples of our God."

At this point, Emelius said, "I awoke, and meditated for a time upon the dream, and then fell asleep again, when I had a continuation of the dream. I thought I saw persons being resurrected from the dead, which caused me to wonder. All at once through the Spirit, or some person, was shown to me the manner of the resurrection, and I thought I had the power given me to bring forth the dead. It was as simple in performance as baptism for the remission of sins. The dead were called forth in the name and by the authority of the Lord Jesus Christ, and I saw them come forth. Those that I saw arise were arrayed in white robes.

"I now awoke, and cannot describe the joy and satisfaction that the Spirit gave me. I rejoiced before the Lord. I saw in my dream no other preachers than Latter-day Saint Elders."[9]

## John Galbraith

Edward J. Wood, President of the Cardston Temple, related John Galbraith's experience during general conference in 1917. John was living on an Indian reservation near a Mormon settlement in Canada when he had the following spiritual manifestation and saw his uncle teaching the gospel.

President Wood said, "This Brother Galbraith had a dream. He said he came to our meeting. He saw in the meeting, in his dream, four or five old Indian chiefs siting on the stand. He knew these Indians were dead and had been for a long time. One of them was his uncle. The highest point on the Rocky Mountains near us was called Old Chief. That was the name of his uncle, the highest chief among the Blackfoot nation.

"He [John Galbraith] said as he went into the audience that this uncle of his told him to come up on the stand with him, and he said he wondered how it was, because this man was dead; he knew this. He went up and he heard his uncle stand up and preach a sermon to the audience there and turn around and say, 'This nephew of mine must be our representative among our people.'

"He [John Galbraith] said the man spoke in a language he could understand, and he marveled at it.

"When he got to this, Brother Galbraith said, 'What have I got to do?'

"He [John's uncle] said, 'You see a book on the table'—and he pointed to a book on the table—'that book contains the history of our people. We are what people call all *dead*, and you are in the life, with the book. It will be told to you what to do.'

He awoke, and after two long years of investigating, he joined the Church."[10]

## William M. Palmer

In this unique experience, William M. Palmer was serving a mission when he left his body and was told by his guide that he needed to teach the gospel—not to spirits in heaven but to two mortal men in his mission area. When William spoke to the men, they were shocked, because although they could hear the elder, they could not see him.

"In 1876, I was laboring alone as a missionary in Michigan. My knowledge of the doctrines of the Gospel was very limited indeed, as I had been of dim sight in my school days, and could not learn to read. I always had, however, great faith in prayer.

"I was laboring among a people called Second Adventists, one of whose cardinal doctrines was 'the sleep of the dead,' as they called it. They believe there is no immortal spirit of man. That we have no intelligence that existed before we were born, neither will it exist after our bodies are laid in the tomb; that the breath is the life, and we cease to exist at death until we are renewed by the resurrection, and then only the Adventists will come forth.

"I had a great desire to know something about the departed spirits, that I might meet this undesirable doctrine with firmness. I was staying at my uncle's house in Sylvester, Mecosta County, Michigan, at the time. I had prayed much on the subject. One day after returning foot-sore and weary from a preaching tour, I lay down to rest in my bedroom. My mind was trying to comprehend the spirit world. All at once I was lost in sleep.

"I seemed to be standing by the bedside; my body lay on the bed upon the right side just as I had laid down, my eyes being closed. I thought I would look and see if everything in the room was natural, for I thought I was dead.

"I moved about at my will, went back to the bed and looked at my body again. Such a feeling of love for my body was in my heart; but I had an assuring feeling that I would get it again in the resurrection. The only sorrow I had was that my body was not among the Saints in Zion.

"Just then, a personage came in the room dressed in a white robe, and said: 'You are wanted to meet some of the brethren in the woods north of Greenville in Maple Valley, to preach to the spirits who know not the Gospel.' [Greenville was about fifteen miles away.]

"I inquired, 'What will become of my body?'

"The answer was: 'They will send it to your family.'

"At the mention of my family a pang shot through my heart, and the messenger noticed it and said: 'Your family will get along; the Saints will look after them.'

"I at once started out. I know not how I got into the street, but I was there and everything looked natural. It was broad daylight. I started for Greenville, and would skip along the road without any effort, part of the time soaring a little above the earth.

"I came to two men who were sawing a log with a crosscut saw, and talking on the doctrine of 'The sleep of the dead.' I went close to them, and I was so anxious to correct them that I spoke and said: 'Don't believe that foolish doctrine any longer. I tell you man has a spirit.'

"They stopped sawing and looked straight at me. One answered: 'I hear you; but where are you?'

"I went within three or four feet of him and said: 'You are looking right at me.' It seemed so strange they could not see me, and I could see them and myself so plainly. I said, 'I am a spirit. You have seen the Mormon preacher who has been around here?'

" 'Yes,' was the answer.

" 'I died a little while ago, and my body is at John Harrington's.'

" 'What shall we do?' was asked.

" 'I have not time to tell you; but go to Henry Thompson, (he was President of the branch), and he will tell you.'

"I went by the nearest way to Maple Valley, soaring above the trees and looking down on them. Everything looked natural and very beautiful. I came to the hill that enclosed Maple Valley, and climbed it easily, with the thought of what a task it would be if I had my body. When I got on top I looked into the valley, and saw hundreds of men and women gathering from all directions to the woods, and when I came to the congregation they seemed to know I was an Elder, for they parted and left an alley for me. I walked to the center. There, standing upon a fallen tree, was President Heber C. Kimball and my father, who died a faithful Elder. They motioned me to come to them and as I arose without any effort, I awoke. This satisfied me, and does to this day."[11]

## Oscar W. McConkie

While serving as president of the California mission, Oscar W. McConkie dreamed that he saw Mark Vest, a member of the Papago Indian Tribe, preaching to members of his tribe in the spirit world.

Mark Vest was the only member of his family who belonged to the LDS Church. He lived in or near Mesa, Arizona, and sometime close to 1950, Mark died while riding on a public bus in Mesa. When his family arranged to have Mark cremated according to Papago custom, Church members objected, saying the Church disapproved of cremation.

Harold Wright, president of the branch in Mesa, called and asked President Oscar W. McConkie to travel to Arizona and speak at the funeral. However, Harold did not explain the complications that had risen between the branch and the family over the issue of cremation.

That night before the funeral, President McConkie dreamed he saw Mark Vest in the world of spirits preaching to people of the Papago tribe. There were hecklers among them who tried to discredit his teaching, saying that Mark was not a Lamanite at all but a Nephite. The protesters did all they could to persuade the people not to listen. But Mark declared that he *was* a Lamanite and a member of the Papago tribe and that he'd been cremated according to their custom. Presented with this, the hecklers subsided, and Mark continued to teach the Papago tribe in the world of spirits.

It wasn't until President McConkie reached Mesa and was told about the problems that had arisen between Church members and Mark's family that he understood the importance of his dream. He told President Harold Wright that it would be all right for Mark to be cremated according to tribal custom.

When President McConkie spoke at Mark's funeral, he explained to those present that he had seen Mark preaching the gospel in the world of spirits. After the funeral service, President McConkie went with the branch president, friends, and family members to witness the cremation of the body according to Papago tribal custom.[12]

## James W. LeSueur

James LeSueur was serving a mission in Great Britain when he received a telegram telling him that his brother, Frank, had been murdered. After asking the other elders to pray for him, James knelt as well and prayed to know why his brother had been taken. The Spirit told him that his brother was needed in the spirit world to teach the gospel to his ancestors.

Before relating his experience, James W. LeSueur addressed those who might question the reality of his experience. He said, "I am a business man, a merchant, not a fanatic, a dreamer, or one subject to hallucinations. I deal principally with the practical affairs of life and consider myself a practical man."[13]

Later in his life, James served as president of the Maricopa Stake and then as chairman of the building committee for the Arizona Temple. James said about this work, "My intense interest in seeing a temple in Arizona, and temple work in general, came mainly from [my] visit to the world of spirits."[14]

James begins his story by giving some background on his relationship with his brother, Frank. James said that while growing up, he and his brother were always close. They worked and played together and never kept any secrets from each other. James said that he and Frank were like Jonathan and David of old.

The boys grew up and Frank went off to attend college. When he returned for a time, James said, "Frank had returned from College a fine specimen of young manhood, having a strong athletic body and a handsome face. . . . He had a smile for all, was especially sympathetic for the unfortunate, the helpless, the wayward. Everyone in the circle of his influence seemed to like him and he was the leader where ever he went. . . . Father had purchased a few thousand sheep and it became Frank's duty to take supplies to the herders away up into the White Mountains, also to keep a supervision over the flocks. He would also carry cheer to the lonely shepherd. They fairly idolized him"[15]

Then Frank returned to college. James was called to go on a mission in 1898, but before he left for Great Britain, he went to Brigham Young Academy (now Brigham Young University) to visit Frank. James recalled, "We spent some pleasant hours together, for we loved each other dearly."[16]

James said it was difficult to leave. "When we were parting, we held each other's hands and we pledged, each to the other, that we would be an honor to our father's name, also [be] faithful to any trust the Lord should put upon us."[17]

James and Frank wanted to do their part to redeem their dead and agreed between them how to accomplish this. It was determined that while James was in the land of their ancestors, he would gather genealogy in his spare time.

As they parted that day, James and Frank had no idea they would never see each other again in this mortal life.

During the next two years, James and Frank kept up a continual correspondence. James stayed busy doing missionary work and then one day received a shocking cable.

He related, "In the Spring of 1900 I was on an island of the Atlantic preaching the Gospel of Christ, and as a side recreation, going into the records of the past and building up a genealogical tree. In the midst of this joyous and soul-satisfying service, I was shocked on receiving the following cablegram from his father. OUTLAWS KILLED FRANK. CAN YOU SAIL ANCHORIA, GLASGOW, THURSDAY?"

James said, "The message stunned me for a moment, then I called the other missionaries around me to pray the Lord [sic] for comfort. I knew that He alone could give it. Each missionary petitioned the Heavenly Father in my behalf, then I prayed as follows:

"Oh, my dear Father in Heaven, Thy will make known to me, for I have tried to be faithful to Thee, for what purpose was my brother taken from me?

"There was a still small voice came in answer, sweet and soul-satisfying saying in substance: 'Thy brother was needed to take care of missionary work among his kindred in the Spirit World.'

"My soul was filled with gladness. All sorrow was gone. He had a greater mission elsewhere. A message from the Spirit world made plain the purpose of his going. He was to have charge of carrying the Gospel message to the Spirits of my relatives who had passed beyond. Just like Jesus, who, while His body was in the tomb, His spirit went to the spirit prison. . . . My brother had a similar mission, only to his kindred. What could be more beautiful than that they should have the privilege of hearing and receiving the glad message of great joy leading to eternal happiness?

"So, I was released from my mission to bring good cheer to my parents. Soon after my return I went to the cemetery and knelt by Frank's grave, where his tabernacle of flesh was buried and looking up into Heaven asked the Lord to let me see him. I was not privileged then, but went away feeling that I would be given the blessing some day."[18]

James soon received the blessing he asked for. It may be that part of the reason his request was granted was due to a blessing he received from President Wilford Woodruff, who promised James, "At the touch of thy Guardian Angel, thy spiritual vision shall be quickened and thou shalt look beyond this world of flesh into a world of spirits and commune with the dead for their redemption."[19]

A few weeks after his return, James and his father went into the mountains to the sheep camps. It was the first trip they had made since Frank's death. James said, "I felt that Frank's spirit was there visiting the camps with us. I wanted to see him, wanted to talk to him, wanted to know what he was doing on the other side.

"My father and I made our bed under the pines and my father retired early, while I went out into the thick grove nearby and knelt in supplication to the Lord for the privilege of seeing Frank and knowing what he was doing. I had full faith that my prayer would be answered. Returning to bed to retire, no sooner did I lie down upon it than my spirit left my body.

"I could see my own and my father's bodies lying upon the bed. By the side of my spirit stood a personage I knew to be my Guardian Angel.

"In a voice of sweetness, he said to me, 'Come go with me.'

"Instantly we began passing through space with a speed of lightening and in what seemed but a few moments, we came into a large and beautiful city, far superior to any I had seen. The buildings were not highly ornamented they stood in simple grandeur. The streets were wide and paved and perfectly clean. They were bordered with trees and flowers, whose beauty could not be told in words. Most of the houses were white and gray, and marble seemed to be the predominant building material. This grand city was one of the cities in which the spirits of those who had died without an acceptance of the Gospel of Christ, were being prepared for its acceptance by missionary service of those who had given faithful allegiance to the Lord, while living in mortality. In the midst of this stood a marble structure of four stories, covering nearly an entire block.

"As we came before it the angel said, 'We will go in here.' Immediately a door opened and a beautiful young lady, whose face was radiant with joy welcomed us. An answer to the query in my mind, the angel said, 'This young lady is a relative of yours assisting as a missionary among the spirits of your kindred, who died without a knowledge of the Gospel. While living in mortality she was killed, and all those you see in this room are your relatives assembled to hear the Gospel taught.'

"I looked over the large, well lighted, well arranged auditorium. I was pleased with its beauty and simplicity. The speakers' pulpit was in the center of the hall, fully twenty feet lower, than where I stood. The seats were arranged in a circle beginning on a level with the speaker's floor, and rising, each tier higher than the other, so that the speaker could see everyone present and they did not seem to be very far away from him. I estimated an audience of ten to twelve thousand seated all in a state of expectancy, as though they were waiting for something with a keen anticipation.

"Presently, as I was looking into the faces of the interesting audience, I heard a person begin speaking to them. He told of the great atonement made by the Savior, of the life and labors of the Lord, Jesus Christ, and His teachings. [Pled] with them to accept of Him as their Redeemer, to repent of their sins and obey the Gospel. If they would do ordinances which they should have attended to in mortality, would be performed for them vicariously (1 Corinthians 15 chap. 29 verse) upon the earth by relatives and friends living in mortality.

"As he finished his discourse, he looked up at me and I saw it was my brother, Frank, who had been killed. His face fairly shown with a radiance of happiness. How my spirit thrilled with rapture! He was supremely happy in this service he was giving. By Frank's side stood a beautiful young lady attired in robes, whiter than the driven snow. She was of medium height with dark hair, a full round face, large brown eyes, and she too was happy beyond language to express.

" 'Who is she?' was the thought that came into my mind.

" 'She is to be Frank's wife,' said the attending angel. Frank was nineteen years of age when he died and was unmarried.

"Frank gave me a smile and a sign of parting. I looked at the audience and saw how pleased they were at the service and the Angel said, 'we will now pass into other rooms.'

"The next large hall contained thousands of people arranged in classes, some with teachers, some studying alone and they were deeply interested in the lessons and books they were considering.

"We then went into another large hall where there were other thousands. These seemed to be of a much lower order of intelligence. They were quarreling and jangling. There was a veritable hub-bub of confusion. I was informed that all in both of these rooms were relatives who were being prepared to be brought to a state where they would eventually be ready to hear and accept the Gospel of the Lord, Jesus Christ. Those in the last room lived upon the earth during the dark ages and at the period of great wickedness and ignorance. It would take ages to redeem them.

"We will now return to your tabernacle of flesh,' said the Guardian angel. With the speed of light we traveled and in what seemed but a few minutes, we stood by the shepherd's camp in the mountains. There were the sheep all huddled together in repose, there the stately pines and at our feet the bed. I took a good look at my own body and at my father. The Angel smiled and nodded and in the twinkling of an eye my spirit returned to my tabernacle of flesh. I called my father from his slumbers and told him of my wonderful experience."

Years later, James related his experience to a congregation. At the end of his talk, James said, "What, 'a dream' did I hear you say? No you are mistaken. My spirit actually left my body, just as surely as Lazarus's spirit left his and later was called back by Jesus. The young lady who greeted us at the door was a cousin of mine, Margaret Odekirk. While living in mortality, she was thrown off a horse, her feet caught in the stirrup, her body drug along the ground as the frightened horse ran for a quarter of a mile. When the horse was stopped, she was dead.

"I did not know of this at the time of my experience, but when I told it to my mother and described the young lady to her, she recognized in the description this cousin.

"The young lady who was to be Frank's wife was a mystery until a Mrs. Kempe came to see us from a neighboring town and told us that her daughter who had died said on her death-bed that she wanted to be sealed in marriage for eternity to Frank LeSueur, that he had appeared to her from the Spirit World and asked that this be done. My brother and this young lady had kept company at college. Mrs. Kempe brought with her the young lady's photo and I recognized at once, the young lady whose spirit stood by Frank as he delivered the Gospel discourses. This was attended to, for my brother-in-law stood proxy for Frank and my sister for Jennie Kempe and they were sealed together as husband and wife, the living for the dead, for all eternity.

"The Bible tells us (Matthew 22:23–30) there is neither marrying nor giving in marriage in heaven. Marriage like baptism is an earthly ordinance and must be attended to here. . . . That one can stand proxy for another is a Gospel doctrine, for did not Jesus stand proxy for us all, the just for the unjust. We too can stand proxy for others and become Saviors upon Mount Zion. . . .

"Besides the evidence above, I have the words of the prophet written down and recorded four years before that I would have the experience of looking beyond this world of flesh into a world of spirits, and I know of a surety that my spirit left my body and visited the Spirit World. It was a grand experience and I thank God for it. Signed, James W. LeSueur."[20]

## Book of Mormon

The Book of Mormon is a divinely translated record that contains many important doctrines regarding the gospel of Jesus Christ. In the latter days, the Book of Mormon will be vital to missionary work—not only on earth but in the spirit world as well. President Ezra Taft Benson said, "Combined with the Spirit of the Lord, the Book of Mormon is the greatest single tool which God has given us to convert the world. If we are to have the harvest of souls that [the President of the Church] envisions, then we must use the instrument which God has designed for that task—the Book of Mormon."[21]

## *Chief Yellow Face*

When Yellow Face, a Kree Indian Chief, visited the spirit world, he was told by his Indian ancestors that he needed to return to mortality to find the book that contained the history of their people.

Edward J. Wood, who later became president of the Alberta Temple, talked about Yellow Face's experience at general conference in 1915. Prefacing his comments, Elder Wood explained that the Kree Indians were a nomadic tribe. Typically, they spent their winters hunting and fishing in one area before returning to Eastern Canada each spring.

One winter, Chief Yellow Face and his tribe traveled from the Eastern part of Saskatchewan to Alberta, Canada. They settled next to the Mormon settlement of Cardston and received permission to camp and trap on Church property. The Krees were a well-educated people, and the Mormons often invited them to attend their meetings and socials.

One day, Yellow Face sent a message to Bishop Parker, asking him to come and visit. When he arrived, Bishop Parker "found a large tent with the heads of these one hundred twenty-eight families there, sitting in a circle."

Yellow Face was sitting in front and told the bishop, "We want you to talk to us. We have been to your meetings. We have been to your parties. You have asked us to dine with you. Now we return the compliment. We want you to come and visit us." He then directed the bishop to go to the center of the circle and speak to them.

President Wood said, "Bishop Parker did not know what to say. He had never been on a mission, wasn't prepared to preach the gospel, but he was struck with the sincerity he saw in the people's faces as they sat in the circle. They were pleased to see him, so he told them about the restoration of the gospel and about our work of colonizing in that country. They did not seem much interested in that.

"After he got through they said, 'Is that all you know about your gospel?'

"He thought and said, 'Well, I believe I have told you all I know.'

"'Well,' Yellow Face said, 'don't you have any books that you talk about?'

"'O yes,' said Brother Parker, thinking of the Book of Mormon.

"'Well, tell us about that book,' the Indians said.

"Brother Parker told all he could. It did not take very long and when he got through, the chief said, 'That is all,' and Brother Parker went home.

"About a week later the chief sent for the bishop again. Brother Parker did not know this time what would be expected of him. But he went and found the same crowd there.

"This time Yellow Face said to Brother Parker, 'When you were here before, I sat there and you stood here. This time I'll stand here and you sit there.'"

Chief Yellow Face then told Bishop Parker about a vision he'd had two years ago.

President Wood remarked, "Mind you, this man never knew anything about our gospel, never knew there was such a thing as visions or heavenly manifestations."

Chief Yellow Face said that during his vision, an angel had told him, "You are going to die, but you won't die all over. When you die, I do not want you to be buried until you get cold all over."[22]

Chief Yellow Face said, "For three consecutive years I have taken my family and gone off into the woods, and when I got there, [I] pitched my tepee and went off in the forest. [This time] I was told by a man [angel] who came there to meet me that I was to lie down under the trees, wrap my blankets around me, and go with him on a journey."[23]

Before he went on this "journey," Yellow Face told his closest friends about the angel and said that he was going to go with him. Yellow Face told his friends to watch his body carefully but not to bury him—even if his body was cold—if there was a warm spot over his heart.[24]

Yellow Face said he then went on his journey. "I went right off, and looked down on my body when I went with this visitor—saw an Indian there wrapped in his blankets, and I wondered how it was that I was living and yet it was I there wrapped in [my own] blankets." When he came back, he said, "The visitor had taught me, oh, so many things—many things you would not believe if I told you, because my own family do not believe them."[25]

President Wood continued, saying that while Yellow Face was gone on his journey "all the other chiefs thought he was dead . . . he was watched for five days and only above his heart was there a small warm place. On the end of the fifth day he came to, and he called all his council together and told them he [Yellow Face] had been into a country where he saw his forefathers, walked with them, talked with them; and they told him we would not yet die, for he would come back to the earth and that he was to send all over the country until he found a people who had a book in which was recorded the history of the many people he had been with in the spirit world; and he said I will give unto you four signs by which you may know the people."

Yellow Face then recounted them: "First, they will not drive you out of their country. Second, you can turn your horses loose and they won't steal them. Third, they will go through your village and they won't rob the virtue of your maiden women. Fourth, they will let you hunt and fish on their domain."

Chief Yellow Face told Bishop Parker, "With my family for two years we have hunted for such a people. You invited us into your meetings. We sat at the table with you in your picnic parties. You have come through our villages; you have not molested our women. We are fishing and hunting today on your Church land. So I tried you, I watched you; we have watched your old men; your young men; we have watched every action of all your people. When I heard you speak it sounded like good music to me and when you said that that was all you had to tell, I thought again, I am disappointed. So I asked if you had a book. You told me you had and told me of your Book of Mormon. That is our book. That is our history, not yours. We want it."

President Wood said, "So Brother Parker went and got the Book of Mormon and brought it back to the Indians. The Indians took it, gave it to the interpreter and had him sit down and read it by the hour."

Chief Yellow Face then told Bishop Parker, " 'It is our book, our history,' and drew out a beautifully embroidered envelope of leather and wrapped it up and took it away."[26]

## Messages Given for Those Still in Mortality

Occasionally, those who visit the spirit world are asked to give messages to people in mortality. Most often, these messages take the form of a rebuke, reprimand, or an admonition to live the gospel more fully. This occurred to Solomon Chamberlin, who was asked by a woman to tell her husband on earth to repent. She also had other messages she wanted Solomon to deliver.

Sometimes the message is one of comfort. During his visit to the spirit world, Heber Q. Hale was asked by a number of people to relay greetings and words of counsel to their loved ones. During his visit (related in chapter eight), Heber says he was stopped by a man, John Adamson. While on earth, John had been murdered, along with his wife and two children, and he asked Heber to tell his other children on earth that they were happy and should not mourn or feel bad about the way they died. John said they were needed on the other side to work on genealogy and the work was of such magnitude that it required all four of them.

Alfred D. Young, whose experience is related in the next chapter, was given several messages for others and was told to do missionary work when he returned to mortality.

When Joseph F. Smith spoke at a funeral of a friend, he declared that even though the woman was now in the spirit world, she would still be able to give counsel to her surviving loved ones. He then added, "In like manner our fathers and mothers, brothers, sisters and friends who have passed away from this earth, having been faithful, and worthy to enjoy these rights and privileges, may have a mission given them to visit their relatives and friends upon the earth again, bringing from the divine Presence messages of love, of warning, or reproof and instruction, to those who they had learned to love in the flesh."[27]

## Sarah Alley

Twenty-year-old Sarah Alley was living in Beekman Town, New York, when she visited the spirit world in February of 1798. While there, several people asked her to deliver warning messages to family and friends.

"I was in my usual health, sitting by the fire side about six in the evening, when, without being sensible of pain or indisposition, I fell, as I was afterwards told, from my chair; and lay apparently lifeless for the space of four or five hours, notwithstanding every mean and effort were used to restore me.

"As I fell, I suppose, I left the body, and found a guide ready to take charge of and conduct me, which I knew to be an angel, and who continued with me during the vision. He first took me to the borders of that lake and pit where there is continual weeping and lamentation."[28]

While there, "a man she knew well urged her to 'go and warn his family and friends to do better than he had done,' before it was too late."[29]

Sarah stated, "I was then conducted by my guide to the place of happiness, where I saw Christ and the holy angels around him, and abundance of people clothed in white robes, but I could not distinguish one from another, so as to know them, being not suffered to enter the kingdom, though I desired the liberty of going in, my guide telling me I must return quickly to the world, for I could not have entrance here. He then conducted me back to my body."[30]

Once Sarah returned to her mortal body and became conscious of her surroundings, she found several people around her. She "pressingly advised them to take warning by her." Then Sarah fainted, and once again her guide took her to the spirit world.

Sarah said the people there "appeared to be sitting, and in a situation of perfect peace and happiness, God sitting above them, and my guide telling me which he was, though he did not converse with me. I also saw Christ, who seemed a little before [in front of] the rest, of whom I begged entrance into that peaceful situation."

Christ told her she had to return to mortality. Some of the people around Sarah asked her to warn their family and friends when she returned to mortality. "They seemingly all joyfully bid me farewell, and my guide conducted me back to my body."[31]

## Notes

1.  Rudger J. Clawson, Conference Report, April 1933, 76.

2.  Brigham Young, *Journal of Discourses*. vol. 3 (London: Latter-day Saints' Book Depot, 1856), 370.

3.  Alvin R. Dyer, *The awakening in the spirit world*, (Courtesy of the Church History Library, The Church of Jesus Christ of Latter-day Saints).

4.  Heber Q. Hale, *A Heavenly Manifestation*, unpublished manuscript in the possession of Ruth W. Gregory, Phoenix, Arizona. Used with permission.

5. Marlene Bateman Sullivan, *Gaze into Heaven: Near-death Experiences in Early Church History*, (Springville: Cedar Fort Inc., 2013), 134.

6. Neal A. Maxwell, *Notwithstanding my Weakness*, (Salt Lake City: Deseret Book, 1981), 55–56.

7. Melvin J. Ballard, *Crusader for Righteousness*, (Salt Lake City: Bookcraft, 1966), 272.

8. Lorenzo Snow, "Discourse by President Lorenzo Snow," *Millennial Star* vol. 56, no. 4 (1894), 50.

9. Emelius Berg, *The Juvenile Instructor*, vol. 31, (1 June, 1896), 343.

10. Edward J. Wood, Conference Report, April 1917, 128–29.

11. William M. Palmer, "Answer to Prayer," *The Contributor* vol. 17 no. 7 (1896): 430–31.

12. Robert James Matthews, *Mark Vest—Papago Lamanite*, (Courtesy of the Church History Library, The Church of Jesus Christ of Latter-day Saints).

13. James W. LeSueur, "A Peep Into the Spirit World," unpublished manuscript in the possession of Ruth Gregory, Phoenix. Arizona. Used with permission.

14. Margie Calhoun Jensen, (compiled), *When Faith Writes the Story*, (Salt Lake City: Bookcraft, 1974), 229–35.

15. James W. LeSueur, "A Peep Into the Spirit World," op cit.

16. Margie Calhoun Jensen, (compiled), *When Faith Writes the Story*, op cit., 229–35.

17. James W. LeSueur, "A Peep Into the Spirit World," op cit.

18. Ibid.

19. Ibid.

20. Ibid.

21. Ezra Taft Benson, "A New Witness for Christ," *Ensign*, November 1984.

22. Edward J. Wood, "An Outstanding Occurrence in Canada," *The Relief Society Magazine*, vol. 4, (March 1917), 135–37.

23. Edward James Wood, Conference Report, April, 1917, 129.

24. Melvin S. Tagg, *The Life of Edward James Wood, Church Patriot*, Master's Thesis, Brigham Young University, 1959), 88–90. Used by permission from Melvin S. Tagg. (Copy on file at Salt Lake City: LDS Church History Library.)

25. Edward James Wood, Conference Report, April, 1917, 129.

26. Edward J. Wood, "An Outstanding Occurrence in Canada," *The Relief Society Magazine*, vol. 4, (March 1917), 135–37.

27. Joseph F. Smith, *Gospel Doctrine; Selections From the Sermons and Writings of Joseph F. Smith,* 11th Edition, (Salt Lake City: Deseret Book, 1959), 436.

28. Trevan G. Hatch, *Visions, Manifestations, and Miracles of the Restoration,* (Granite Publishing: Orem, 2008), 25–26.

29. Richard Lyman Bushman, "The Visionary World of Joseph Smith," *BYU Studies* vol. 37 no. 1 (1997–98): 189.

30. Trevan G. Hatch, *Visions, Manifestations, and Miracles of the Restoration,* op cit., 25–26.

31. Richard Lyman Bushman, "The Visionary World of Joseph Smith," *BYU Studies* vol. 37 no. 1 (1997–98): 189.

*Chapter Eleven*

# Different Spheres in the Spirit World

THERE ARE TWO main regions in the spirit world: paradise and spirit prison (Alma 40:12–14). People are taken to paradise if they died before the age of accountability (eight years of age) or if they were baptized on earth and remained obedient to God during their earthly life. Paradise is a term that simply means a place of departed spirits. Paradise first appears in the Bible in the Savior's utterance from the cross when He promised the penitent thief He would see him that day in paradise (Luke 23:43).

The spirits in paradise and in spirit prison will dwell apart until the resurrection. A great gulf separates the two areas. Nephi mentions this, saying, "A great and a terrible gulf divideth them" (1 Nephi 12:18). Jesus also talked about this separation when He gave the parable of the rich man and Lazarus, saying there was a great gulf fixed so that people could not pass (Luke 16: 19–26).

Paradise is a vast place with many different areas containing the same cross-section and diversity of race and creed that exists now upon the earth. Parley P. Pratt spoke of this when he said, "There are many places and degrees in that world as in this."[1]

People usually associate with those they feel comfortable with, and this will hold true in the spirit world. There—as on earth—people are free to choose where they want to live and do so according to personal likes and dislikes. The righteous will dwell with people of comparable natures, and those less valiant will choose to live with those of similar character. "For intelligence cleaveth unto intelligence; wisdom receiveth wisdom; truth embraceth truth; virtue loveth virtue; light cleaveth unto light; mercy hath compassion on mercy and claimeth her own" (D&C 88:40).

President George Q. Cannon said, "There will be just as much distinction between spirits there as you find between spirits here. Those who have made good use of their opportunities here will have the benefit of their diligence and faithfulness there. Those who have been careless and indifferent . . . will find themselves lacking there."[2] This quote suggests that our circumstances in paradise will be due to our own making and will be a result of how we lived while in mortality.

"The spirit will awaken there with the same tendencies to religious belief and righteousness or the lack of it that they have here," said Apostle Alvin R. Dyer. "The murderer shall not be in the same place with the righteous; nor the adulterer, with the virtuous. Nor shall the honest be with the liar and dishonest. It would be folly in the justice of God for it to be otherwise."[3]

After his visit to the spirit world, Heber Q. Hale said it was clear that "the inhabitants of the spirit world are classified according to their lives of purity and their subservience to the Father's will. . . . Particularly was it observed that the wicked and unrepentant are confined to a certain district by themselves the confines which are as definitely determined and impassable as the line marking the division of the physical from the spirit world—a mere film, but impassable until the person himself has changed."[4]

## Samuel H. Webster

While at the temple, Samuel H. Webster was granted a vision and saw the celestial, terrestrial, and telestial kingdoms.

"Therefore on the morning of Feb. 26, 1934, That while I was waiting in the Celestial room to go through the Vale of the Temple meditating on the glorious privileges and blessings of the Temple work I beheld the Glorious sight of the Celestial Kingdom of God in a flash of a most Glorious light beyond all description and Bro. James E. Talmage appeared to me in the flash of the light and said to me Bro. Webster you have lived the law of the Word of Wisdom about as nearly and consistently as it is possible for any man to do, but you have overlooked some of the most important features of the blessings you are entitled to. You read the 19th verse of the 89th Sec. of Doc & Cov. Then read the references to the 76 Sec—5–10 verses also the last 5 verses of the same Sec.

"These are some of the many blessings you are entitled to.

"I also saw the glories of the Terrestial [*sic*] and Telestial Kingdoms. Then I had the glorious privlgae [*sic*] of hearing Apostle James E. Talmage as it were delivering the following short but pointed discourse apparently to a congregation of spirit beings. I also heard as it were a multitude singing praises to God for the glorious light of truth that had come to them; I also heard a repitation [*sic*] of the same service the following two mornings the 27–28 of Feb. 1934. The same time in the morning session.

"In reference to my seeing the glories of the Terrestial [*sic*] and Telestial Kingdoms I have not the language nor space to attempt an explanation of the grandeur and glorious manifestations of power that I beheld which was beyond all description in the Terrestial [*sic*] world many of those spirit beings were identified with a bright light as those who would have received the truth, had they have had the opportunity of having been taught the gospel while in the flesh. I also observed that Apostle Orson F. Whitney was addressing this vast concourse of spirit beings, and I recognized the truth as Christ told the brother of Jared that his spirit was represented exactly in form and personage as he was here in the flesh while on the earth.

"The Telestial World with its millions and billions of spirit beings were beyond all comprehension to imagine their magnitude in numbers of glory and power."[5]

## Alfred D. Young

After Alfred D. Young was baptized on September 16, 1841, he was ordained an elder by his brother William. A few days after his ordination, Alfred and his brother were sitting in front of William's house, talking about the gospel, when Alfred decided to go to the woods to pray. While praying, he had an extensive vision of the spirit world and saw the celestial, terrestrial, and telestial kingdoms, as well as the place where the unrighteous dwell. Alfred writes,

"As we walked, he [William] continued to talk on the principles of the Gospel and the gifts that had been made manifest, but I had little to say as I was in deep meditation. When we had retired about 200 paces from the house into a piece of timber I saw a light burst through the tops of the trees a little southeast of me. I was wrapped in a light which far exceeded the light of the sun. A personage appeared clothed in a white robe exceeding in brightness the light of the sun. . . . He was dressed in a white robe but his feet were bare.

"My nature could not bear the presence of this glorious person and I sank to the ground. My brother, walking by my side, as he afterwards stated, saw my countenance change and that I was sinking to the ground. He took hold of my clothes [illegible writing] and let me gently down. This much I do know that my spirit went out of my body and stood just over it and I gazed at it and my brother standing by it. Whether my spirit was commanded to come out of my body by the personage in whose presence I was I know not.

"The personage or angel said to me 'Follow thou me.' He ascended upwards in the direction from whence he came and I followed him. He took me into the presence of God the Father and of his son Jesus Christ, with the exception there was a veil between us; but I saw them seated on a throne."

Alfred said he found himself holding sheaves of wheat and that "there was an altar on my left hand and also one directly in front of me. The one on my left appeared to be about three feet in height; the one in front about eighteen inches. I laid the sheaves of wheat that were in my hands on the altar to my left as an offering to the Lord. I bowed myself on my knees on the altar in front of me which was also in front of the throne.

"I prayed, 'God the Father in the name of his son, Jesus Christ, to accept of the offering I had laid upon the altar.' While I prayed, the veil was removed and I stood upon my feet. Jesus arose and stepped from the side of His Father and came near where I stood. I was in their presence and I gazed upon their glory.

"Jesus then said to me, 'Your offering is accepted and wouldst thou know the interpretation thereof?'

"I replied, 'Yea, Lord.'

"The angel, my conductor said, 'Look' and I saw, as it were, an innumerable company that had come up from all nations, kindreds and peoples around the throne of God, and they fell down and worshiped him and gave glory to him.

"Jesus then said, 'These are they that shalt be the means of bringing unto my Father's kingdom, and this is the interpretation of the offering thou has laid upon the altar.'

"Jesus continued to speak and showed me many things pertaining to His Father's kingdom. One thing I am at liberty to tell, the others I am not.

"He told me look and said that there were neither sun nor moon to give light but the Father and his Son were the light that lighted all the kingdoms of the world. This is all of the vision of the Celestial world that I am permitted to write.

"The angel said again to me 'Look.' I looked I beheld the lesser kingdom, typified by the moon. It received its light from the Celestial kingdom and the inhabitants thereof seemed to exceed those of the Celestial world but the glory was not equal to that of the Celestial. I saw many angels descending and ascending between the Celestial and Terrestrial worlds. I saw the angels descending and ascending between the Terrestrial and Telestial world and administering to the inhabitants of the latter. This is the end of the vision concerned the Terrestrial world.

"The angel said again to me, 'Look,' and I looked and saw another kingdom and the inhabitants thereof seemed to exceed those of both the Celestial and Terrestrial worlds. I saw the angels descending and ascending between the Terrestrial and Telestial worlds and administering to the inhabitants of the latter. The glory of the Telestial seemed great but not as great that of the Terrestrial.

"The angel said again to me, 'Look.' As I looked, I beheld another world in which the inhabitants appeared to be less in number than in any of the three worlds that had before been shown me. Perhaps I might call it a kingdom. It was neither one of light or of glory; but one of suffering. It was shaded with darkness. It appeared to be a pit; and a thick darkness of smoke ascended upwards as far as I could see. The inhabitants appeared to be suffering beyond anything I can describe."

After this, Alfred was shown a panorama of events. He saw John the Baptist, and Peter, James, and John laying their hands on the head of Joseph Smith as if ordaining him. Alfred saw the Saints gather and that when persecutions arose, many left the Church. The angel then showed Alfred where the ten tribes of Israel were gathered in a vast multitude on the shore of a body of water.

Next Alfred was shown a great light in the eastern sky, which signified the coming of the Savior. The light grew larger as it approached earth, and within the light was the Savior with numberless angels and Saints. As Christ drew nearer, many wicked people on earth bowed and acknowledged that Jesus was indeed the Christ. Satan was cast, out and the old earth fell away, leaving a new earth with its multitude of inhabitants and a great temple.

Alfred said of the temple, "It was beautiful beyond my capacity to describe."

He also saw the great work to redeem the dead. "Enough was shown me in this Temple to give me some idea of the great work to be done in the Millennium." He was admonished to do missionary work when he returned to his physical body.

Alfred saw numerous relatives who lived approximately 250 miles east of where he lived.

The angel said, "Behold thy brethren. They have heard of the Gospel but there is no one to preach it to them. Go and preach it to them and they will believe. Go and behold I will be with you."

Then it was time for Alfred to return to mortality. He said, "The angel, my conductor, said, 'follow me,' and he conducted me back to where my body lay on the ground. I saw it and my brother still standing over it. He had watched over it, as near as he could judge, some three or four hours. My Spirit entered into my body and I stood upon my feet, and the angel still stood by me.

"When [I was] in the body, he showed me the remnants of Israel, of the seed of Lehi scattered over the southern portions of North America. I saw many of my brethren, the Elders of Israel go forth among them and finish the gospel and many were baptized. I saw a great Prophet raised up among the remnants and he went forth with [illegible writing] among them preaching the Gospel. Many were converted and baptized and great faith was exercised among them.

"After the angel left me I turned to my brother and called him by name and related to him all that I had seen and heard. Some of it he doubted.

"I said to him, 'Brother William, you shall yet be witness to the truth of all I have said.' At these words he fell to the earth as if he were dead."

Alfred felt impressed to touch him. "I did as directed and he arose to his feet, bore testimony to the truth of what I had seen and continued to bear that testimony until his death.

"My brother William afterwards stated that he saw no person with me nor heard any conversation although he stood near me. But . . . while it appeared as if dead, it was manifested to him that I was in a vision.

"I feel to record a tribute of thanks, honor and praise to God, my Heavenly Father and to his Son, Jesus Christ, for the glorious things that have been revealed to me in these visions. I regret my inability to properly represent them for I want of a proper comprehension of language to express my ideas, but as far as I am able, I desire to leave them on record as a testimony to my posterity and to the word of the goodness, power and majesty of God and of the truth of the great Latter-day work, as inaugurated by Joseph Smith [illegible writing] for the final redemption of the earth.

"In the year 1858 I was counseled by Apostle George A. Smith to write this vision and have it placed upon the church record. I have employed Elder James A. Little to write this as scribe with the design of having it filed in the Church Historian's Office. [signed] Alfred D. Young."[6]

## Spirit Prison

The second part of the spirit world is referred to as spirit prison, although the term *prison* doesn't mean the same thing as a prison on earth. It is referred to as a prison simply because people who reside there are not allowed to leave and enter paradise until certain conditions have been met. It is chiefly a place of learning and waiting—not a place of suffering. *Spirit prison* is not to be confused with *hell*, which refers to the place where the wicked will live after the final judgment. Both paradise and spirit prison are temporary abodes where spirits will stay until the resurrection and the final judgment.

There are two categories of people who reside in spirit prison. The first category consists of people who have not yet fully received the gospel. People who did not have the opportunity to hear the gospel during their earthly life will have a chance to learn about the gospel while in spirit prison. If they choose, they can accept the gospel and be baptized. However, they must remain in spirit prison and will not be able to progress until all of the necessary ordinances are performed vicariously on earth by living proxies in the temple (see D&C 138).

The second category of people living in spirit prison consists of those who acted wickedly while on earth. "The spirits of the wicked, yea, who are evil—for behold, they have no part nor portion of the Spirit of the Lord; for behold, they chose evil works rather than good; therefore the spirit of the devil did enter into them, and take possession of their house. . . . Now this is the state of the souls of the wicked, yea, in darkness, and a state of awful, fearful looking for the fiery indignation of the wrath of God upon them; thus they remain in this state, as well as the righteous in paradise, until the time of their resurrection" (Alma 40:13–14).

The people in this category will also have an opportunity to learn about the gospel. If they desire, they may repent of their sins and receive forgiveness and salvation though Jesus Christ. The Lord gave President Joseph F. Smith a vision about how this work would be accomplished. President Smith was pondering the words of Peter, who said the Son of God preached unto the spirits in prison, when he received the vision of the redemption of the dead.

President Smith said, "I perceived that the Lord went not in person among the wicked and the disobedient who had rejected the truth, to teach them; but behold, from among the righteous, he organized his forces and appointed messengers, clothed with power and authority, and commissioned them to go forth and carry the light of the gospel to them that were in darkness" (D&C 138:29–30).

Until the death of Jesus Christ, paradise and spirit prison were completely separated from each other by a great gulf, but after the Savior's death, the gulf was bridged and the Lord sent righteous spirits to teach the gospel to those in prison. When spirits in prison repent and have their saving ordinances performed, they will be able to join the righteous in paradise.[7]

## Ann Booth

Ann Booth's vision of the spirit world is one of the earliest on record in LDS history. It impressed Wilford Woodruff so much that he wrote it down in her own words in his journal on March 12, 1840. In her vision, Ann saw the people in spirit prison shouting for joy when they realized the prison doors had been opened and that missionaries had arrived to teach them the gospel.

"Being Carried away in a vision to the place of departed souls I saw prision one above another vary large and builded of Solled [solid] Stone. On arriving at the door of the uppermost prision, I beheld one of the 12 Apostles of the Lamb who had been martered in America Standing at the door of the prision holding a key with which he unlocked the door and went in and I followed him.

"He appeared to be of a large size thick set, Dark hair Dark eyes and eyebrows of a smileing Countenance, and on his head was a Crown of Gold or sumthing brighter. He was Dressed in a long white robe with the sleeves plaited from the Sholder to the hand. Upon his breast were four stars **** apparrently like gold and a golden girdle about his loins. His feet were bear from above the ancles downwards, and his hands were also bear. As he entered the prision he seemed to stand about 3 feet from the floor (which was of Marble) as if the place was not worthy for him to stand upon. A vary brilient and glorious light Serrounded him while the rest of the Prision was dark. But his light was peculiar to himself and did not reflect upon others who were in the Prision who were surrounded with a gloom of darkness.

"On the right hand near the door stood John Westley who on seeing the glorious Personage raised both hands and shouted Glory, honor, Praise, and Power be ascribed unto God and the Lamb forever and forever. <u>Deliverance has Come</u>. The Apostle then Commenced to Preach the Baptism of repentance for remission of Sins and the gift of the Holy Ghost by the laying on of hands, when the hundreds of Prisoners gave a shout with a loud voice Saying Glory be to God forever and ever.

"The marble floor was then removed and a river of water Clear as Cristle seemed to flow in its place."

Sister Booth said that at this point, the Apostle began to baptize people in the river, including many of her relatives.

"The next he Baptized was my Grandfather (Edmund Whitehead) and the next was my uncle (John Whitehead) and the next was my sister (Elizabeth Olland) and next Joseph Lancashire and next Samuel Robinson and then next was my own Mother. All these had lived and died Methodist and I had been personally acquainted with them all."

Sister Booth witnessed the Apostle baptizing hundreds of people and then confirming them. She said, "Then instantly the darkness dispersed and they were all Surrounded and envelloped in A Brilient light such as surrounded the Apostle at the first. . . . My Grandfather then Came to me and blessed me saying the Lord bless thee forever and ever."

He then said, "'Art thou come to see us deliverd?' My mother then came to me and clasped me in her arms and kissed me three times. . . . I then awoke out of the Vision and felt so happy and overjoyed that I knew not how to remain in bed."

Sister Booth woke her husband, and they went to the Bible and began looking up scriptures, reading what Peter had to say about the spirits in prison. Sister Booth said that although she and her husband had previously not understood many scriptures, they now made perfect sense because of the new knowledge and information the vision had given them.

Sister Booth concluded by saying, "I would further state that at the time I had this vision I had never herd of the Death of David W. Patten whom I have since learned was one of the Twelve Apostles of the Latter Day Saints in America and was slain in the late persecution in the fall of 1838. But in the Vision I knew it was an Apostle who had been slain in America.

"Perhaps many will think lightly of this vision But I hereby sollemnly testify that I actually Saw and herd in a vision what I have here related and I give my name and set my seal in witness to the Same well knowing that I must stand before the Judgement seat of Christ and answer for this Testimony."[8]

## Solomon Chamberlin

Solomon Chamberlin had two spiritual manifestations, which will both be related here. His first experience occurred in 1807, when he was still a teenager. At that time, Solomon had a frightening vision of hell that convinced him he needed to change his ways. He made an effort to change, but for many years, he alternated between living righteously and reverting back to his sinful ways. The first manifestation occurred as follows:

"Soon after God called me by a vision of the night. At this time I was in the 19th year of my age; while in my slumbers I saw that the day of judgment had fully come, and all nations were assembling to hear their doom; we were drawn by an irresistible power. I tried hard to stop but could not, for I shudered at the thought of coming before God to give an account of my wicked life. . . . I trembled at the thoughts, and expected every moment to begin my eternal torment; but to my great joy and surprise a man came to me and said, you may go back to yonder world and have one year longer to prepare for death in, and if you are not prepared at the expiration of one year, you, or one of your neighbors by the name of Ephraim Herger will come to this place of torment.

"I then awoke and found it to be a vision of the night; I was in a great sweat, groaning and crying to God for mercy, and glory to

God, it had its desired effect; I thought if I did not repent and lead a better life I should soon die and go to hell."

After Solomon's vision, he resolved to change his evil ways. "I began to consider on my past life and give way to conviction. I felt the need of religion, and having Christ for my friend . . . I thought I would go to some professor and enquire what I should do to be saved, for I was so ignorant of the plan of salvation that I knew not what to do to be saved. . . . I heard of a methodist prayer meeting about five miles distant which I attended. . . . I began to vent my feelings to God and cry with a loud voice . . . and I felt a peace of mind. . . . From this time till the year 1816 I passed through various scenes, sometimes happy in God, and oftentimes I had to mourn my apostacy from God."

For years, Solomon went back and forth between believing in God and obeying the commandments, and living wickedly. Then Solomon began praying that God would show him the true church. Solomon was living in Massachusetts in the fall of 1819 when he was visited by an angel and had his second vision.

Solomon related, "One Monday morning while at work in my shop I was taken with a weakness through my whole system, the cause I could not tell, I was well in body but the exercise increased more and more, and in awful awe and glory of the presence of Christ filled the room, and my mind was wonderfully drawn up into heaven; I felt a very still and quiet spirit, for to stand still and see the salvation of God; my appetite for food was wholly taken away from me, and my body as completely satisfied as if just refreshed with food and drink; it seemed I required no literal food for I ate but little of any kind for almost seven days. . . .

"My exercise increased till Wednesday in the afternoon I was in a continual scene of prayer all this while, I now cried with a vocal voice and said Holy Ghost teach me from the eternal world, and I prayed in faith. That moment there was a departed spirit entered [sic] the room.

"The reader may wonder how I should know that there was a departed spirit in the room and could not behold it with my bodily eyes, but I could behold it with the eyes of my spirit; it was a woman that formerly had belonged to the society, and died happy in the Lord; she was the wife of Daniel Arnold, she saluted me with these words, 'don't you remember the exhortation that I gave you while on my dying bed.'

"I now knew her in a moment, and said yes, that I do sister spirit.

"Now the exhortation was this, she exhorted me to live more obedient to God, and not live so light and trifling—be more sober and watchful, &c. the spirit says "go thou and do likewise,' tell my husband he must repent and do his first works, or where I am he never can come. This man had backsliden [sic] from God, in heart, and had a name to live in the church.

"The spirit gave me a message for a number of the society of like cases, and gave me a charge to be faithful and go and deliver them at their meeting on Sunday—she said they all would be their [sic] and that I should have an opportunity, and speak in the power and authority of the holy Ghost.

"The state of the society was now opened to my view, and I had a spirit of discernment, and could discern the sandy foundation that many of them were building on. I now fell on my knees and gave thanks to God for his condescension to unworthy me, and while lifting up my soul to God it appeared to me that I saw my Saviour [sic] stand before me with the bible in his hand, and said to me this is the book—live in the spirit that this was wrote and you shall shine in the eternal world on high. I now felt joy and peace that is 'unspeakable and full of glory.' I opened my bible that lay on my bench, and it was opened to my understanding with such glory as I never saw before, and my exercise increased, for I now felt my message to be from the eternal world."

The following Sunday, Solomon and his wife attended church. After the lesson, Solomon stood and addressed the congregation:

"I have a message from the eternal world to deliver to this people; and . . . it came not by my own imagination neither is it a phantom of the brain, but I will tell you how I came by it."

Solomon then related his experiences. Afterward, he delivered the message Sister Arnold had given him to her husband and others. "I then turned and delivered my message to several others, while some wept, others mocked."

Afterward, Solomon said, "I now felt the glories of the invisible world to fill my soul. . . . I feel wholly given up to follow the lamb of God withersoever [*sic*] he shall be pleased to lead me."[9]

# Notes

1. Parley P. Pratt, *Journal of Discourses* vol. 1 (London: Latter-day Saints' Book Depot, 1855), 9.

2. George Q. Cannon, *Gospel Truth; Discourses and Writings of President George Q. Cannon*, vol. 1, comp. and ed. Jerreld L. Newquist (Salt Lake City: Deseret Book, 1974), 76.

3. Alvin R. Dyer, *The awakening in the spirit world*, (Courtesy of the Church History Library, The Church of Jesus Christ of Latter-day Saints).

4. Heber Q. Hale, *A Heavenly Manifestation*, unpublished manuscript in the possession of Ruth W. Gregory, Phoenix, Arizona. Used with permission.

5. Samuel H. Webster, *Faith-promoting collection*, (Courtesy of the Church History Library, The Church of Jesus Christ of Latter-day Saints).

6. *Alfred Douglas Young Autobiographical Journal 1808-1842*, unpublished manuscript, (Provo: L. Tom Perry Special Collections, Harold B. Lee Library, Brigham Young University), 3–12.

7. Bruce R. McConkie, *Mormon Doctrine*, (Salt Lake City: Bookcraft, 1966), 762.

8. Scott G. Kenney (Edited), *Wilford Woodruff's Journal, 1833-1898 Typescript*, vol. 1, (Midvale: Signature Books), 475–77.

9. Solomon Chamberlin, "Solomon Chamberlin's Missing Pamphlet," *BYU Studies* vol. 37, no. 2 (1997-1998): 131–37.

*Chapter Twelve*

# One Eternal Round

OUR LIVES CAN be said to be one eternal round. Although we cannot remember it, we lived once with God in a premortal existence, and when our time on earth is done, we will return again to that heavenly sphere.

When we came to earth, Heavenly Father put a veil over our memories. Brigham Young spoke about this, saying, "It has also been decreed by the Almighty that spirits, upon taking bodies, shall forget all they had known previously, or they could not have a day of trial—could not have an opportunity for proving themselves in darkness and temptation, in unbelief and wickedness, to prove themselves worthy of eternal existence."[1]

Once our time on earth is done and we return to the spirit world, the veil of forgetfulness that was placed on us at birth will be stripped away. Our memories will be restored and we will be able to remember our life in the premortal world. George Q. Cannon said, "Memory will be quickened to a wonderful extent. Every deed that we have done will be brought to our recollection. Every acquaintance made will be remembered. There will be no scenes or incidents in our lives that will be forgotten by us in the world to come."[2]

Brigham Young said that when we go to the spirit world, we will "see that [we] had formerly lived there for ages, that [we] had previously been acquainted with every nook and corner, with the palaces, walks, and gardens." We will then say, " 'O my Father, my Father, I am here again.' "[3]

Before we came to earth, some of us made promises—either to other people or to God. However, because of the veil that blocks our memory, those promises were forgotten once we arrived in mortality. A few people who visited the spirit world had the veil temporarily withdrawn long enough to remember promises they made in the premortal existence.

## Niels P. L. Eskildz

When Niels P. L. Eskildz saw into the spirit world, he remembered promises he had made in his premortal life. As a young boy, Niels had been terribly deformed in an accident. People were repelled by his appearance, and he was shunned by society. Because of his severe handicaps, it was difficult for Niels to earn even a meager living. Niels often felt miserable about being poverty-stricken and ostracized. Then he had a vision. In it, Niels was allowed to recall promises he had made before coming to earth. Remembering these promises instantly and dramatically changed Niels's attitude about his difficult circumstances. His experience was written by George C. Lambert:

"It was not a single scene that [Niels] beheld, but a series of them. He compares them to the modern moving pictures, for want of a better illustration. He beheld as with his natural sight, but he realized afterwards that it was with the eye of the spirit that he saw what he did. His understanding was appealed to as well as his sight. What was shown him related to his existence in the spirit world, mortal experience and future rewards. He comprehended, as if by intuition, that he had witnessed a somewhat similar scene in his pre-mortal state, and been given the opportunity of choosing the class of reward he would like to attain to. He knew that he had deliberately made his choice. He realized which of the rewards he had selected, and understood that such a reward was only to be gained by mortal suffering—that, in fact, he must be a cripple and endure severe physical pain, privation and ignominy. He was conscious too that he still insisted upon having that reward, and accepted and agreed to the conditions.

"[Niels] emerged from the vision with a settled conviction that to rebel against or even to repine at his fate, was not only a reproach to an Alwise [sic] Father whose care had been over him notwithstanding his seeming abandonment, but a base violation of the deliberate promise and agreement he had entered into, and upon the observance of which his future reward depended.

"Whatever opinion others may entertain concerning the philosophy involved in this theory, is a matter of absolute indifference to Niels. He does not advocate it; he does not seek to apply it to any other case; but he has unshaken faith in it so far as his own case is concerned. . . . He has derived comfort, satisfaction, resolution and fortitude from it. He has ever since [the vision] been resigned to his affliction, and, though never mirthful, is serene and composed and uncomplaining. He has always felt that the vision was granted to him by the Lord for a wise and merciful purpose—that he might, through a better understanding of his duty, be able to remain steadfast thereto."[4]

## Lorena Washburn Larsen

Destitute and unable to provide for her children by herself, Lorena Larsen struggled with rebellious feelings toward a husband who visited her only rarely. Because her husband was gone the majority of the time, Lorena decided not to have any more children until her husband could live with and provide for them. However, she changed her mind after going to the spirit world and learning about promises she had made in the premortal existence.

"In 1897 I was so sorely tried; my husband was not able to provide for his family and our children had to go without things to make them comfortable, and many things were trying me. I felt that although I struggled to provide to the best of my ability, it was not sufficient, and I felt that my husband, though such a splendid man, yet was partial in his dealings with his families, and that he was unsympathetic with my part of the family. I became discouraged. To rear my family practically alone was a sore trial.

"And so I decided that I would have no more children unless my husband could come and live with us as a father should live with his family, and give us the love and sympathy which every family should have. I was really rebellious about having any more children under the present circumstances.

"One night I dreamed that I passed out of the body, and was surprised to find that there wasn't a greater change between this life and the life hereafter. I looked at my body lying on the bed and I fully realized that I was really in the Spirit World.

"Immediately my whole life passed before my mind like a panorama, and I had a knowledge of what the Lord approved of, and what he did not approve. I was surprised to find that some of my human weaknesses which I myself had condemned, were of little or no consequence. The only thing that was held against me was the rebellious feeling I had had about having more children.

"I there and then knew that before I came to earth I had promised to be the mother to a certain number of children, and there were two or three of that number that were still unborn. I knew exactly the number then, but after I came to myself again I could not remember definitely.

"When the realization of the fact came upon me that I had failed to keep my promise with the Lord, had failed to fill the measure of my creation, I was in hell. The torment of my mind was past description. I wrung my hands in awful agony. I looked down at my body on the bed, my spiritual hand took hold of my mortal hand, and I said, if I had only known, if I had only known.

I wondered how long this torment of soul would last, and immediately I knew it would never end. I looked in every direction, I could see there was no end to time and space.

"The walls of the house did not obstruct the view. In a north-westerly direction from where I stood I saw a man afar off, coming through the air toward me. He was small at first, but increased in size as he came nearer. I knew when I first saw him that he was a good man, and that when he came I could tell him everything.

"Presently he stood beside me and I told him my story. I said it was not because I did not want more children, but because they were not properly cared for.

"He said, 'Don't you know that was a trick of the adversary to cut you short of your glory.'

"I knew as I stood there that he spoke the truth, and as I wrung my hands I said, 'I know, I know.'

"I then asked him, 'Is there no way that I can get back into my body and fill the measure of my creation?

"He said, 'Only by faith and much prayer.'

"I said, 'Faith is a gift of God and I will pray.'

"I got down on my knees and began to pray earnestly, and the next thing I knew I awoke, there was a tingling sensation all through my body, like when a leg or arm goes to sleep. I got up and knelt by the side of my bed, and offered such a prayer of praise and thanksgiving to the Lord as I had never offered before, and I promised the Lord I would publish my experience as far as possible, so that no other woman should have such an awful experience when passing to the Spirit World. It seemed to me that it was hell of the worst type.

"I have had two children since that time, but have never been sure that there was not another one that I should have had.

"The Lord has been so good to me. He has rewarded me in the quality of my children a thousand fold, for the trials I have passed through."[5]

# Notes

1. Brigham Young, *Journal of Discourses* vol. 6 (London: Latter-day Saints' Book Depot, 1859), 333.

2. George Q. Cannon, *Gospel Truth, Discourses and Writings of President George Q. Cannon,* vol. 1, comp. and ed. Jerreld L. Newquist (Salt Lake City: Zion's Book Store, 1957), 77.

3. Brigham Young, *Journal of Discourses* vol. 4 (London: Latter-day Saints' Book Depot 1857), 268.

4. George C. Lambert (compiled), *Treasures In Heaven*; 15th *Book of the Faith Promoting Series*, (Salt Lake City: George C. Lambert, 1914), 21–22.

5. Floy Isabell Larsen Turner, *Lorena Eugenia Washburn Larsen, A Mother in Israel*, (Courtesy of the Church History Library, The Church of Jesus Christ of Latter-day Saints), 65–67.

*Chapter Thirteen*

# A Life-Changing Experience

PEOPLE WHO VISITED the spirit world became more cognizant of God's eternal plan for mankind and came back to mortality changed because their experiences gave them a more complete knowledge of the gospel.

After seeing into the spirit world, a number of people who did not belong to The Church of Jesus Christ of Latter-day Saints at the time of their experience became convinced of the truth of the gospel and were baptized.

After pondering his experience, Mr. Pettersson realized it had been a gift from God. Prior to his glimpse into the spirit world, he had felt sure he was on the correct path, but afterward—newly humbled—Mr. Pettersson decided he needed to learn more about the gospel. He went to see Mr. Carlsson, a man he had previously scorned for being a Mormon. Mr. Carlsson gladly taught him the principles of the gospel of Jesus Christ, and soon afterward, Mr. Pettersson, his wife, and his older children were baptized.[1]

Sanford Porter was another man who became converted after his visit to the spirit world, although it took many years before he actually joined the Church. Sanford resisted baptism at first because he'd been told during his spiritual manifestation that the true gospel was not yet on earth. Even after the missionaries patiently explained that the true Church had *not* been on earth at the time of Sanford's vision and that it had since been restored, Sanford was still hesitant. To convince him it took another spiritual manifestation, where the guide who had previously escorted him to the spirit world confirmed to him that the gospel had been restored to earth. Shortly after, Sanford was baptized, along with his wife and two of his children. Afterward, he spent much of his time teaching the gospel, bringing many to a knowledge of the truth.[2]

David John's life was changed when he was allowed to see into the spirit world, not once but twice. After seeing Christ in all His glory, David returned to mortality with a profound knowledge of what was important in life. His experience gave him a deep and unwavering testimony, and afterward he dedicated himself to The Church of Jesus Christ of Latter-day Saints. David served a mission and for the rest of his life did what he could to build up the kingdom of God.[3]

One of the most important pieces of knowledge a person can receive is an assurance that Jesus is the Christ. During his experience, David B. Haight witnessed a full and detailed panorama of Christ's life, which further strengthened his already deep-rooted testimony of the Savior and His mission. Elder Haight said, "I cannot begin to convey to you the deep impact that these scenes have confirmed upon my soul." He said his experience gave him an unshakable testimony of the eternal mission and exalted position of Jesus Christ, the Redeemer of all mankind.[4]

One of the most common changes that occurs after visiting the spirit world is for the visitor to lose all fear of death. After Charles V. Anderson had his manifestation, he was no longer afraid of dying. Although Charles was told during his experience that he would soon fall seriously ill, he wasn't disturbed at the prospect. Charles said, "I was so full of happy and peaceful thoughts. I knew I would have to pass through a severe sickness, even close to death, but I did not feel the least alarmed. . . . If I ever had any fear of death, it has entirely passed away, for now I know and understand."[5]

Lorena Wilson also lost her fear of dying. She stated, "Since that happy experience my former fear or dread of death has left me entirely. I have not mourned and cannot mourn for the dead, though I sympathize with the sorrowing. An abiding assurance had taken possession of me that the dead have only gone to a better place by far than this—a place of peace and happiness and of opportunity for advancement."[6]

A miraculous healing was one of the after-effects of Luana Anderson's experience. For most of her young life, Luana had suffered from palsy and been unable to attend church or school. But after visiting the spirit world, she was healed enough she could participate in regular activities outside the home such as school and church.[7]

Unlike Luana, Niels Eskildz, who had been crippled as a young boy, was not healed of his disability. Shunned by society, he felt miserable and lonely. However, when Niels was allowed to see into the spirit world, he remembered that before coming to mortality, he had been told that if he wanted great blessings in the next life, he would need to endure great hardships in mortality. Niels had agreed and knew that to rebel now at his circumstances—no matter how dreadful—would violate the agreement he had entered into during his premortal life. Remembering the covenants he had made brought peace to his soul and allowed him to become reconciled to his hardships. Even though his life continued to be difficult, Niels was determined to meet his trials without further complaint.[8]

David Lynn Brooks also experienced a newfound peace after his spiritual manifestation. David was mourning the death of his wife when she appeared to him. He was then allowed to glimpse into the spirit world. David was so happy to see his wife and awed by the spirit world that great tears of happiness rolled down his cheeks.⁹

When he was nineteen, Solomon had a terrifying vision of hell. At this time in his life, he often indulged in drinking, fighting, and swearing. However, his fearsome vision convinced Solomon he needed to change. He felt sure God allowed him this experience so he would mend his ways. Solomon tried to live more in tune with the spirit, but in the coming years, he fluctuated between living righteously and backsliding to his sinful ways. Twelve years later, when he was thirty-one, an angel of God appeared, exhorting Solomon to be more obedient and giving him another vision, which showed him the reward he would receive if he lived righteously.¹⁰

Philip Haskins was another man who had difficulty following God's commandments, but after visiting the spirit world and receiving light and knowledge, he changed his ways. Unfortunately, his vision did not affect a lasting change. Years later, Phillip wrote that he "was overtaken with anger, and I gave way to it." The account ends by reporting that Phillip died in black despair, twenty years later.¹¹

After visiting the spirit world, a number of people became interested in temples and temple work. When he was a young man, James W. LeSueur saw into the spirit world. Later in life, he served as president of the Maricopa Stake and then as chairman of the building committee for the Arizona Temple. James said about this work, "My intense interest in seeing a temple in Arizona, and temple work in general, came mainly from [my] visit to the world of spirits."¹²

Ruby Lee Vaughn also learned about the importance of temple work when she went to the spirit world. Ruby states, "As I saw others busy and happy, I felt that I wanted to go back [to mortality] and get my temple work done, so I could return and work in the celestial kingdom, so I knelt and prayed for another chance to return to earth." Ruby was allowed to return to mortality, and stated, "I know that I will strive to live to return there, [to the temple] and strive to always say 'no' to all that is not pure and holy."[13]

After his visit to the spirit world, John Powell underwent a change and was filled with a desire to alter his lifestyle and prove himself worthy of entering the temple to receive his endowments and to do ordinance work for the dead. At first, however, John was hampered by the glories he had seen in his vision. Immediately after returning to mortality, John said, "I had no more desire to live. I would rather pass away for I was so filled with the scenes of bliss that I had no more desire for this world as it is." The Lord then allowed him to see his wife in the temple. This made John decide to live more righteously so he could receive the blessings of the temple.[14]

When William D. Pelley saw the splendor of the spirit world, he had a difficult time returning to mortality and taking "up the burden of earthly living again." Then, speaking in third-person, William humorously talked about the changes his visit had wrought in his life: "I know that the experience has metamorphosed the cantankerous Vermont Yankee that was once Bill Pelley, and landed him onto a wholly different universe that seems filled with naught but love, harmony, health, good humor, and prosperity."[15]

People who were allowed to glimpse the spirit world were always profoundly affected as they learned more about the purpose of mortality. They came back armed with knowledge and fortified with a renewed sense of purpose, which convinced many to live more righteously and to change their priorities from worldly ones to spiritual ones. Their lives were forever changed when they saw that spending time and money to obtain a larger home, fancy vehicles, or clothes or taking expensive vacations would not earn them a place of glory in the next life. Instead, they learned that diligently seeking after righteousness would bring them great joy, unparalleled happiness, and increased glory in the next phase of their existence.

The people in this book saw for themselves what Isaiah meant when he said, "Wherefore, do not spend money for that which is of no worth, nor your labor for that which cannot satisfy" (2 Nephi 9:51; see also Isaiah 55:2). Life is not about acquiring power or possessions, because none of that can be taken to the next life. Obedience to God's commandments, showing love to others, and doing good works are the only assets that will follow us to the spirit world. "For what is a man profited, if he shall gain the whole world, and lose his own soul? or what shall a man give in exchange for his soul?" (Matthew 16:26).

We can use the experiences contained in *The Magnificent World of Spirits* to expand our understanding of what lies ahead and, if we choose, to reassess our lives. These accounts urge us to use our time in mortality wisely and make good choices that will benefit us throughout the eternities. We should seek for opportunities to serve others and to improve ourselves by developing divine qualities of kindness, generosity, sympathy, mercy, love, and charity. "Verily I say, men should be anxiously engaged in a good cause, and do many things of their own free will, and bring to pass much righteousness" (D&C 58:27).

## Notes

1. J. M. S., "In the World of Spirits," *The Latter-day Saints' Millennial Star*, vol. 79 no. 1, (1917): 1–7, 11–13.
2. Nathan Tanner Porter, *Reminiscences [ca.1879]*, (Courtesy of the Church History Library, The Church of Jesus Christ of Latter-day Saints).
3. *Biography of David John*, Leonard J. Arrington Collection, (Logan: Utah State University).
4. David B. Haight, "The Sacrament—and the Sacrifice," *Ensign*, November 1989, 59-61.

5. Charles V. Anderson, *Faith-promoting Collection 1882-1974*, box 1, folder 3, (Courtesy of the Church History Library, The Church of Jesus Christ of Latter-day Saints).

6. Lorena Wilson, *Life Sketch and Experiences of Lorena A. Wilson,* (Logan: Special Collections, Milton R. Merrill Library, Utah State University, 1932).

7. Charles R. Woodbury, *Faith Promoting Experiences of Patriarch Charles R. Woodbury,* (Courtesy of the Church History Library, The Church of Jesus Christ of Latter-day Saints).

8. George C. Lambert (compiled), *Treasures In Heaven*; *15th Book of the Faith Promoting Series*, (Salt Lake City: George C. Lambert, 1914), 21–22.

9. Duane Crowther, *Life Everlasting*, (Salt Lake City: Bookcraft, 1967), 59-60. Used with permission of Horizon Publishers & Distributors, Inc.

10. Solomon Chamberlin, "Solomon Chamberlin's Missing Pamphlet," *BYU Studies* vol. 37, no.: 2, (1997–1998): 131–37.

11. Philip Haskins, *A Sketch of the Experience of Solomon Chamberlain to Which Is Added a Remarkable Revelation or Trance of His Father-in-law Philip Haskins,* (Provo: L. Tom Perry Special Collections, Harold B. Lee Library, Brigham Young University, 1829), 140.

12. Margie Calhoun Jensen, (compiled), *When Faith Writes the Story*, (Salt Lake City: Bookcraft), 1974), 229–35.

13. Norma Clark Larsen, *His Everlasting Love*, (Bountiful: Horizon Publishers, 1977), 136–38. Used with permission of Horizon Publishers & Distributors.

14. John Powell, *Autobiography and Journal, 1849 June-1901 Apr.,* (Courtesy of the Church History Library, The Church of Jesus Christ of Latter-day Saints).

15. William Dudley Pelley, "Seven Minutes in Eternity," *Faith-promoting collection 1882–1974,* Box 2, Folder 104, (Courtesy of the Church History Library, The Church of Jesus Christ of Latter-day Saints).

*Chapter Fourteen*

# Life Will Continue

ECAUSE OF THE Atonement of Jesus Christ, we know we will live again. Jesus taught, "For as in Adam all die, even so in Christ shall all be made alive" (1 Corinthians 15:22). Apostle Melvin J. Ballard declared, "After death, that which existed before and independent of the body will continue, until through the resurrection of the earth body the union of spirit and matter will take place, providing the power and ability to touch and know all realms. We are reaping what we have heretofore sown, so shall we hereafter reap what we now sow. To guide us to success for now and hereafter the Gospel of the Son of God was given. I know as well as I see you now, that I shall see you hereafter the same individuals, that as God is without the beginning of days or end, so also is the offspring of man."[1]

Although most of us will never have the dramatic spiritual manifestations in mortality that these people did, we can use their experiences to give us valuable insight into the plan of salvation. Each of these experiences confirms to us that mortality is just one step on the pathway of an eternal existence. When our bodies die, our spirits will go to the spirit world to await the resurrection, when they will be reunited with our bodies—never to be separated again. Although life is precious and we should appreciate our time here, life continues on after death. "Therefore the grave hath no victory, and the sting of death is swallowed up in Christ" (Mosiah 16:8).

These stories also allow us to feel the power of God's love, which can encourage us to live in such a way that we will be able to return to His presence.

## What Happens after Death

The experiences in *The Magnificent World of Spirits* teach us many things about death and the post-mortal life.

- **At death, the spirit rises out of its physical body.** People can look back to see their body.
- **A guide appears.** After death, we are not left alone but are met by a spiritual guide—often a loved one—to ease our transition into the spirit world.
- **Life continues, feeling natural and real.** The spirit lives on with the same personality and characteristics it had in mortality. The spirit world will seem familiar, normal, and real.
- **Clothing is most often described as white robes.** However, other types of clothing are also worn.
- **Our eyesight will be greatly enhanced.**
- **Communication will be different.** Although we will be capable of speech, spirits have the ability to read another person's thoughts. The language there appears to be universal.
- **Spirits are able to move about easily.** Vast distances can be covered quickly and usually without effort.
- **Our ability to learn, comprehend, and remember will be vastly increased.**
- **We will be reunited with family and loved ones.** Relationships continue beyond the grave. We will be reunited with departed family members and friends.

- **We may be allowed to see Heavenly Father and Jesus Christ.** Many people report seeing Jesus, and a few report seeing God the Father.
- **We may be able to see ancient prophets and apostles, as well as modern-day Church leaders.** A number of people saw the Prophet Joseph Smith, as well as other ancient and modern Church leaders.
- **Light is an integral feature of the spirit world.** Light permeates the spirit world and appears to originate from God the Father and Jesus Christ.
- **People will experience intense feelings of love, peace, and happiness.**
- **Music is an important part of life in the spirit world.**
- **The spirit world is beautiful beyond description.** The spirit world is filled with lovely gardens, shrubs, trees, foliage, and flowers.
- **There are animals, fowls, and insects in the spirit world.** People reported seeing birds, fish, butterflies, and all kinds of domesticated and wild animals.
- **There are individual homes and all types of other buildings.**
- **There are cities in the spirit world.**
- **There are magnificent temples.**
- **People are busily engaged in a variety of labors and activities.**
- **Many spirits are involved in genealogical work.**
- **Learning continues.** Education is an important, ongoing process. Adults and children will be provided with educational opportunities.
- **The gospel will be taught in the spirit world.** Missionaries will teach those who want to learn more about Jesus Christ and His Church.
- **Agency—the power to choose—will continue to be a God-given right.** People will have the right to listen or ignore and to accept or reject the message of the gospel.

- **The Book of Mormon.** The Book of Mormon will continue to be an integral part of the holy scriptures.
- **The two main regions in the spirit world are paradise and spirit prison, both of which have different areas.** Where a person goes after he dies depends on the kind of life he lived while on earth.
- **Spirit prison.** People in spirit prison will stay in this area until they accept the gospel and have their ordinance work done. Missionaries will be sent to spirit prison to teach those who want to learn about the gospel.
- **The veil of forgetfulness that was placed on us at birth will be removed.** We will be able to remember our life in the premortal existence and any promises we made there.
- **Those who visit the spirit world exhibit an increased spirituality upon their return to mortality.** Most resolve to live more righteously so they can receive the blessings they saw in the spirit world.

## Enduring to the End

All of us have a mission to fulfill while on earth. We can be guided by the Holy Spirit to know what our individual mission is and to fill it to the best of our ability if we obey the commandments and live worthily. Our goal during mortality is to fill our mission; press forward, continually doing good works; and endure to the end. We will be richly blessed and filled with joy if we can accomplish these things. In Mosiah 2:41, we read, "And moreover, I would desire that ye should consider on the blessed and happy state of those that keep the commandments of God. For behold, they are blessed in all things, both temporal and spiritual; and if they hold out faithful to the end they are received into heaven, that thereby they may dwell with God in a state of never-ending happiness."

Enduring trials patiently can be seen as a test of our faith. The Book of Mormon prophet Alma teaches us, "I do know that whosoever shall put their trust in God shall be supported in their trials, and their troubles, and their afflictions, and shall be lifted up at the last day" (Alma 36:3).

Although we all make mistakes, we can repent and continue to progress because of the Atonement of Christ. While in this mortal estate, we are encouraged to overcome our faults and to develop divine characteristics of love, mercy, and charity. As we strive to increase in light and knowledge, we can improve ourselves so that when we lay our physical bodies down and move on to the spirit world, we will be able to partake of the glories awaiting us there. "Wherefore, ye must press forward with a steadfastness in Christ, having a perfect brightness of hope, and a love of God and of all men. Wherefore, if ye shall press forward, feasting upon the word of Christ, and endure to the end, behold, thus saith the Father: Ye shall have eternal life" (2 Nephi 31:20).

## Lay Up Treasures in Heaven

Reading about people's visits to the spirit world reminds us that mortality is transitory and fleeting and that we ought to use our time to prepare for and be worthy of glory in the next life. As we ponder these experiences, we may feel the whisper of the Spirit bearing a sweet testimony that these stories are true. All of them testify that Heavenly Father and His Son, Jesus Christ, are divine Beings who love us and are aware of our lives here on earth.

The eyes of our understanding can be opened as we learn that money and material things are not important. What truly counts is doing all we can to help those around us, including tending to the sick, depressed, and needy. The Lord declared, "Seek not for riches but for wisdom, and behold, the mysteries of God shall be unfolded unto you, and then shall you be made rich. Behold, he that hath eternal life is rich" (D&C 6:7). Then, when this life is over, we may return to God's presence and the glories awaiting us there.

The experiences in this book give credible evidence that life continues beyond this life and are remarkably similar to the near-death experiences contained in *Gaze into Heaven: Near-death Experiences in Early Church History*. All of these experiences testify that Heavenly Father loves us, that He watches over us, and that He wants us to return to live with Him once more.

We should not take these experiences lightly but use them as a witness of the truth. "And now, my brethren, I would that, after ye have received so many witnesses, seeing that the holy scriptures testify of these things, ye come forth and bring fruit unto repentance. Yea, I would that ye would come forth and harden not your hearts any longer; for behold, now is the time and the day of your salvation. . . . For behold, this life is the time for men to prepare to meet God; yea, behold the day of this life is the day for men to perform their labors. . . . I beseech of you that ye do not procrastinate the day of your repentance until the end; for after this day of life, which is given us to prepare for eternity, behold, if we do not improve our time while in this life, then cometh the night of darkness wherein there can be no labor performed" (Alma 34:30–33).

## Notes

1. Melvin J. Ballard, *Crusader for Righteousness*, (Salt Lake City: Bookcraft, 1966), 108.

# Acknowledgments

ANY THANKS TO Monica Miles, Stella Chase, Leah Hansen, and John Wells, who read the manuscript and gave many helpful suggestions. I also want to thank Holly Horton for her editorial expertise and McKell Parsons, my exceptionally talented editor, for all of her help. As always, I want to thank my wonderful husband, Kelly, for his loving support.

# About the Author

ARLENE BATEMAN WAS born in Salt Lake City, Utah, and grew up in Sandy, Utah. She graduated from the University of Utah with a bachelor's degree in English. Marlene is married to Kelly R. Sullivan and lives in North Salt Lake, Utah. Her favorite hobbies are gardening, camping, and reading—not necessarily in that order. She loves animals and, although she has four cats and two dogs, is constantly trying to talk her husband into letting her get a few more. Her animal friends keep her company while she writes.

Marlene has been published extensively in magazines and newspapers and has written a number of nonfiction books, including *Gaze into Heaven: Near-death Experiences in Early Church History* and *Heroes of Faith.* She also enjoys writing mysteries. Her first novel, a mystery/romance, is the bestselling *Light on Fire Island.* She also wrote *Motive for Murder, A Death in the Family,* and *Crooked House.*